Economic and political institutions in economic policy

Economic and political institutions in economic policy

edited by

V.A. Muscatelli

Manchester University Press
Manchester and New York
distributed exclusively in the USA by St. Martin's Press

Published by Manchester University Press
Oxford Road, Manchester M13 9NR, UK
and Room 400, 175 Fifth Avenue,
New York, NY 10010, USA

Distributed exclusively in the USA
by St. Martin's Press, Inc.,
175 Fifth Avenue, New York, NY 10010, USA

British Library Cataloguing-in-Publication Data
A catalogue record for this book is available from the British Library

Library of Congress Cataloging-in-Publication Data
Economic and political institutions in economic policy / edited by
V.A. Muscatelli.
p. cm.
'Lectures delivered in the University of Glasgow, as part of the 1993 programme of Stevenson Lectures in Citizenship'—Pref.
ISBN 0–7190–4993–8
1. Economic policy. 2. Economic policy—International cooperation. 3. Institutional economics. I. Muscatelli, Vito Antonio.
HD87. E247 1996
338.9—dc20 96–28198
CIP

ISBN 0 7190 4993 8 *hardback*

First published in 1996

00 99 98 97 96 10 9 8 7 6 5 4 3 2 1

Typeset in Hong Kong
by Graphicraft Typesetters Ltd, Hong Kong
Printed in Great Britain
by Bookcraft (Bath) Ltd

Contents

List of figures and tables

Figures

Tables

Contributors

Alberto Alesina is Paul Sack Professor of Political Economy at Harvard University and a Fellow of the National Bureau of Economic Research. He has held appointments at Carnegie-Mellon University and visiting appointments at the International Monetary Fund and The World Bank. He has published widely in the area of political economy and monetary and fiscal policy design, including *Partisan Politics, Divided Government, and the Economy* (1995, with Howard Rosenthal).

Anthony B. Atkinson is Warden of Nuffield College, Oxford University. He was previously Professor of Economics at the Universities of Essex, UCL, LSE, and Cambridge. He has edited the *Journal of Public Economics*, and has written widely on social issues and on public economics. His books include *Lectures on Public Economics* (1980, with Joseph Stiglitz), *Unemployment Benefits and Unemployment Duration* (1985, with John Micklewright), and *Poverty and Social Security* (1989).

James M. Buchanan is Distinguished Professor of Economics and Advisory Director of the Center for the Study of Public Choice, George Mason University. He was previously Professor of Economics at the Universities of Tennessee, Florida State, UCLA, and Virginia Polytechnic Institute. He was awarded the Nobel Prize for Economics in 1986. His books include *The Limits of Liberty* (1975), *The Reason of Rules* (1985, with G. Brennan), *The Economics and the Ethics of Constitutional Order* (1991).

Anton Muscatelli is Daniel Jack Professor and Head of the Department of Political Economy, University of Glasgow. He is joint editor of the *Scottish Journal of Political Economy*. He has published widely in the areas of monetary economics, applied macroeconomics and international economics, and previous books include *Macroeconomic Theory and Stabilisation Policy* (1988, with Andrew Stevenson and Mary Gregory).

Tommaso Padoa-Schioppa is Deputy Director-General of the Banca d'Italia. He was previously head of the money market department of the Banca d'Italia, Economic Adviser to the Italian Treasury, and General Manager Economic and Financial Affairs of the EC Commission. He has published widely in the area of monetary economics. His recent works include *Efficiency, Stability and Equity* (1987), and *The Transition to EMU in the Maastricht Treaty* (1994, with Lorenzo Bini-Smaghi and Francesco Papadia).

Gordon Tullock is Karl Eller Distinguished Professor of Economics and Political Science at the University of Arizona. He previously held appointments at the Universities of South Carolina, Virginia, Rice, and Virginia Polytechnic Institute. He has published widely in a number of areas of economics. His books include *The Calculus of Consent* (1962, with James Buchanan), *The Social Dilemma: The Economics of War and Revolution* (1974), *Trial on Trial: The Pure Theory of Legal Procedures* (1980).

Preface

This volume consists of a series of public lectures delivered in the University of Glasgow as part of the 1993 programme of Stevenson Lectures in Citizenship. The Stevenson Lectures, which are held annually, are funded by a bequest from Sir Daniel Macaulay Stevenson, Bt, who was Chancellor of the University from 1933 to 1944. In 1993 the Department of Political Economy had the opportunity to organize a lecture series which brought a number of distinguished economists to the University. Each invited speaker was asked to deliver a public lecture which would examine the role of institutions in economic policy, and the lectures were intended to be accessible to a non-specialist audience.

On behalf of the Department of Political Economy and the Stevenson Lectureship Committee, I would like to thank all the contributors to this volume for their stimulating contributions, and for the helpful discussions which they conducted with members of the Department while visiting Glasgow. Finally, I am also grateful to Mrs Eileen Reynolds for her invaluable help in organizing the lecture series, and to Manchester University Press for their efficient production of this volume.

1 *Anton Muscatelli*

Introduction

Until recently, the study of economic phenomena and the study of the institutional framework within which economic decision-making takes place have developed in a largely independent fashion.

Of course, economists traditionally used to pay close attention to the institutional context within which they built their behavioural models and sought to make policy prescriptions. However, in most cases, institutions were treated as exogenous constraints on economic behaviour, and no formal analysis was provided of how institutions themselves might respond to economic phenomena. In a sense, the treatment of institutions was analogous to the treatment of time in Newtonian mechanics: if not quite fixed and immutable, institutional behaviour was generally treated as exogenous when modelling economic behaviour.

Similarly, economists and other social scientists who were mainly concerned with the study of the detailed process of decision-making within institutions (be they governments, government agencies, or other entities in charge of economic policy-making) tended to concentrate exclusively on how the particular institutional context helped to shape policy, paying less attention to the ways in which economic phenomena in turn might affect the incentive structure facing the institution.

Newer developments in the theory of economic policy have tended to place greater emphasis on the two-way interaction which exists between economic phenomena and institutions which play a role in formulating and executing economic policy. At a general level, the common theme which runs throughout research of this type is that policy-makers and bureaucrats are treated as economic agents (or groups of economic agents) who pursue their own objectives, which may or may not coincide with those of the wider community or the electorate whom they represent, and who are constrained by the (imperfect) control exercised on them by their electors or employers. It is worth remarking that the framework adopted in this literature is quite flexible. Economic agents are considered to be rational and are assumed to maximize their own objectives. However, their objectives need not be narrowly defined so as to include only economic variables, so that non-economic factors relating to the social and political environment can also be considered. Thus, one side-effect of these developments has been that of strengthening links between economics and the other social sciences.

The potential conflict between individual and social objectives in turn leads to several important and related questions, which economists and political scientists working in this area have tried to address. First, if there is a conflict which emerges between the pursuit of self-interest on the part of political and economic institutions and the wider community, what mechanisms can be devised to ensure that society's welfare is maximized? Second, do certain institutional structures provide more appropriate incentive constraints for the efficient pursuit of economic policy? Third, what are the potential conflicts between the pursuit of economic welfare and other social and political objectives, such as democracy and social justice?

Of course, many of the analytical tools used by economists working in this research area are by no means novel. The use of game-theoretic analysis, for instance, is reminiscent of similar applications in the areas of welfare economics and industrial economics. Indeed, many of the issues confronted by the 'new theories of economic policy' are well known to economists: externalities, the provision of public goods, non-co-operative games, principal-agent problems. What is new is the context: the use of economic theory to analyse what was previously regarded as an institutional datum. The tools of analysis are often modern, but the type of analysis which emerges is one which is firmly in the old 'political economy' tradition.

The objective of the current series of Stevenson Lectures was to bring together a number of experts from various fields of economics to provide contributions in this broad area. The lectures were specifically designed to be accessible to a wide audience, including non-specialist economists. The contributions cover a wide range of subjects, but the unifying theme of the book is the two-way interaction between institutions and economic policy. Each of the chapters highlights the importance of studying economic incentives when we consider the design of economic and political institutions.

In the first lecture, presented in Chapter 2, Anthony Atkinson looks at the way in which the setting of a social justice objective in the form of an official poverty line might affect policy-making. Thus, the theory of economic policy is deployed to examine the interaction between the setting of traditional objectives of economic policy and broader social objectives.

Atkinson begins by looking at the absence of an explicit poverty policy goal in the United Kingdom. Tracing the history of social welfare policy in the UK, he concludes that social welfare schemes since the publication of the Beveridge Report have not made any attempt to relate the scale of welfare payments schemes to some definition of a poverty line. This is in contrast to the European Community, where a poverty standard has been established on which statistics are published. It is also in contrast to the United States, where since 1964 a poverty line has been established and monitored over time. However, even in the USA, there is no explicit link between welfare payments schemes and the poverty line objective, which raises the issue of whether the establishment of a standard actually could have an impact on economic policy.

Atkinson analyses the potential impact of an explicit social policy target using the new theory of economic policy, taking into account the way in which such targets could affect policy-makers' objectives, and hence their policy actions. He uses a two-party political model along the lines of Alesina (1987; 1988), where each party declares a policy on total income and an anti-poverty programme (which are assumed to be negatively related), and each party has a probability of being elected given society's own preferences concerning the two policy targets, and given random voter turnout. In these circumstances, the announcement of a poverty target, as a precommitment over one area of policy, may affect the outcome of the electoral and policy process. Two conclusions follow. First, the party with a lesser preference for social spending may actually benefit from the imposition of an explicit target because it precommits itself to some level of social spending, and will act so as to prove its willingness to maintain benefit levels. Second, the party with a preference for greater social spending will not benefit electorally from such a precommitment, but it might yet benefit because, in case of electoral defeat, an outcome which ensures a minimum level of social provision will be more acceptable to it.

Furthermore, Atkinson notes that more moderate policy outcomes constrained by a poverty line might be Pareto-superior to fluctuations between two more extreme policy positions which would be taken up by the two parties without such a constraint. One can think here, as Atkinson notes, of a poverty line as a way to discipline short-sighted voters, who may vote for lower benefits and taxes despite some long-term desire to see a reduction in poverty. This would, however, go against the basic assumption of voter rationality usually adopted in the 'new political economy' models (see Persson and Tabellini, 1990). An alternative possibility would be to argue that moving between two extreme positions on taxation and benefit levels involves some social waste, as policy-makers spend considerable time and resources over-hauling the benefit and taxation system on a periodic basis.

Finally, Atkinson considers whether an acceptable poverty line standard could be agreed for the UK. Despite the computational and political difficulties in agreeing on a target, he notes that it should not be too difficult to draw up a poverty standard such as the one in the USA, if its sole purpose is to provide a statistical device to monitor government performance rather than as a benchmark for actual benefit payments. At the very least, it would give some minimum measure of the scale of the problem, and it would put poverty on a par with closely monitored macroeconomic policy targets.

In Chapter 3, Alberto Alesina examines in detail the interaction between the formulation of macroeconomic policy and political institutions in the USA, looking at ways in which the electoral process both influences and constrains governments' policy decisions. This in turn yields lessons for the design of political institutions.

Alesina starts off with some basic facts which may be observed from the US business and electoral cycle, and outlines an economic model which can explain these observations, based on earlier work by the author, and on a recent volume which synthesizes much of the earlier work in this area (Alesina and Rosenthal, 1994). The key notion behind this general model of the US political system is the existence of a polarized two-party system, where the two parties place different weights on output and unemployment fluctuations on the one hand, and inflation on the other. The Republican Party places greater weight on inflation than unemployment, while the Democratic Party does the opposite. This explains the presence of a partisan macroeconomic policy cycle (formalized in Alesina, 1987) which has been detected in the USA, and which is in contrast to the Nordhaus (1975) conventional theory of a political business cycle. Here Alesina refines this notion of polarized government further by introducing a role for mid-term elections, that is elections which take place between presidential elections. While the outcome of the presidential election has an important impact on the formulation of macroeconomic policy, 'divided government' – that is a Congress in which the president's party is in minority or does not have a clear majority – will act as a moderating influence on such macroeconomic policy. Alesina observes that there is a clear tendency for voters to swing away from the party of the presidential incumbent in mid-term elections. This 'mid-term' cycle can be interpreted as middle-of-the-road voters exerting a moderating influence on the presidential incumbent. This does raise the question as to why balancing (through 'split voting') is less marked in congressional elections which coincide with presidential elections. Alesina attributes this incomplete balancing to the presence of uncertainty in the outcome of the presidential election which will reduce tactical (split) voting.

The author then reports on some empirical tests of this general model which he and other colleagues have recently produced. Alesina and Rosenthal (1995) test these theories of the partisan cycle and find confirmation for the existence of a post-election partisan cycle effect. This arises from the combination of a polarized two-party system and some degree of nominal wage rigidity due to staggered wage contracts, where some nominal wages are set ahead of elections in conditions of uncertainty regarding the electoral outcome and hence the stance of future policy. They also find concrete evidence of a mid-term cycle. A final issue which is considered is whether electoral outcomes, especially in presidential elections, are affected by the performance of the economy in the incumbent's period of office. This notion of 'competence' was analysed by, among others, Rogoff and Sibert (1988) and Persson and Tabellini (1990). Alesina suggests that the evidence points to voters rewarding an incumbent who has presided over high growth and punishing an incumbent when growth is low. He also suggests that there seems to be no evidence that voters seek to understand whether high or low growth has been due to competence (or the lack of it), or due to fortuitous factors outside the control of the administration. However, one of the difficulties in disentangling various effects is that the small number of observations available to such studies only allow simple models to be tested.

One important issue which arises from this reconstruction and interpretation of US experience is whether it offers any lessons to other countries in matters of institutional design. Alesina sees the US experience of divided government as being close to that of minority or coalition governments in many other parliamentary democracies. The main problem which arises from divided government is that it may also lead to 'gridlock', and in the arena of fiscal policy to problems of deficit control. However, there is a potential trade-off, as stronger governments in pure majoritarian systems with no mid-term elections (such as the UK) may experience little or no 'gridlock', but may suffer excessive partisan cycles.

The chapter by Gordon Tullock analyses the problem of rent-seeking inside organizations, looking at both large private companies and public organizations. The starting point of Tullock's analysis is the idea that employees in both private and public organizations who wish to plot a successful career path will engage in activities which will not necessarily maximize the organization's declared objective or, more generally, social welfare. An employee wishing to be successful in an organization will generally engage in 'conformist' behaviour, so as not to alienate her or his immediate superiors. This may also lead to individuals using resources to gather information about the internal workings of an organization, rather than gathering information about the external environment in which the organization operates. The former activity is generally of little use to, say, a firm wishing to maximize profits (unless it also led to an improvement in efficiency), while the latter is seen as a more productive activity from the whole organization's point of view. The problem with the latter activity, as Tullock notes, is that the gains from this might be very small for the single employee in the middle of an organization. An employee wishing to put forward an idea which might improve the performance of the whole organization would gain little from such activity unless he persuaded his superiors to adopt it (without alienating them), and while retaining some credit for having proposed the idea.

Could an incentive structure not be put in place to avoid these 'perverse dynamics' inside complex organizations and bureaucracies? This depends, as Tullock notes, on the discipline which shareholders exert on large private organizations, and the ability of governments to monitor the performance of bureaucracies. Arguably in both cases the monitoring is less than perfect, and the control exerted may be weak. But Tullock argues that while very large firms may be able to survive for a considerable period of time while underperforming, especially where they have some market power, eventually the market will force a major shake-up to occur. We also do observe, in private companies, schemes such as profit-related bonuses aimed at creating the right incentives, and as Tullock notes, modern decentralized firms are more subject to direct market discipline than the old vertically integrated large corporations. In contrast, the incentive structure is much weaker in government organizations.

When looking at the performance of government, Tullock distinguishes between elected politicians and unelected bureaucrats. The first category is subject to some electoral discipline, albeit one which is limited by the availability of information available to voters, and the strength of parties as unitary partisan organizations. Here Tullock contrasts the US and UK political systems, with the latter being seen as a much stronger bipolar, partisan, political system. However, looking back to the evidence presented by Alesina in his chapter, it seems apparent that the USA can still be characterized in terms of a bipolar system.

In any event, Tullock's main concern is the almost total absence of a similar discipline in the case of permanent, unelected bureaucrats. He recognizes the difficulties in finding appropriate targets which could be monitored for many public organizations, but gives an example of how such incentives could be set up in one particular case, that of the US Federal Reserve. Linking the salaries of Federal Reserve Board members to the achievement of price stability would be one incentive scheme. This type of optimal contractual solution to principal-agent problems has in fact been widely studied in the theoretical literature (see Laffont and Tirole, 1993). The application of optimal contracts to the case of central bank performance has also been studied (see Walsh, 1995; Persson and Tabellini, 1993), and an incentive scheme along these lines has been adopted in New Zealand. But with a few exceptions, such contracts are rarely observed, which tends to back Tullock's pessimism about the viability and effectiveness of such arrangements.

Finally, Tullock looks at ways in which decentralized government and electing local government officials might lead to some improvements in accountability, although he recognizes that such schemes may also be rather imperfect, given the costs of information gathering on the part of voters. In addition, it is well recognized that decentralization can bring about a trade-off between accountability and efficiency (see, for instance, Seabright, 1994), and indeed these considerations are central to the debates about the optimal size of local government authorities and fiscal federalism.

The chapter by James Buchanan discusses how democratic majoritarian settings may encourage the pursuit of special interests, and looks at possible reforms of political institutions to avoid the domination of such interests. Buchanan argues that, although the 1980s saw some reversal in the role of the state in the market, political interference in market relationships is still pervasive in the Western democracies. Buchanan sees the root of the problem as residing in the fact that coalitions of special interests in majoritarian democratic systems may lead to the exploitation of the few by the many, through the pursuit of special interests.

Buchanan contrasts the operation of a democratic polity with that of the market. Exploitation of a free market participant is not possible because, at least in an ideal market, there is the possibility of exit from market interactions. But how could the notion of 'exit' be extended to the political sphere? Like Tullock, but for different reasons, Buchanan sees decentralization and 'competitive' federalism (in the sense that economic agents and resources are free to move between them) as a solution. But while Tullock stresses the notion of greater accountability in a decentralized political system, Buchanan sees this as a way of introducing competition between political units and of reducing the power of special interest groups.

There might also be an argument for moving away from majority rule in legislative assemblies towards greater unanimity, which would make it more difficult for special interest coalitions to work effectively. Buchanan illustrates how majoritarian politics might not lead to an optimal solution if, as he assumes, there is a potential low-taxation-for-all equilibrium which is Pareto-superior to other equilibria in which alternating majorities manipulate tax and transfers in favour of their section of society.

In a sense, as Buchanan stresses, his proposition relies on placing economic characteristics on an equal footing with personal characteristics when designing constitutional limits. At present most democracies find it unacceptable to discriminate between the taxation and benefit treatment of different classes of citizens on the grounds of personal characteristics (e.g. gender, race), and he argues that this concept should be extended to people with different economic characteristics (income, wealth, occupational status, industry, and so on). He sees the incorporation of a principle of generality as central to a liberal order, and as an effective way to rule out 'special case' taxation and transfers for sections of the population or protected industries.

Overall, Buchanan presents a perspective on constitutional design which is in sharp contrast to those who have argued that distributional considerations are not an obstacle to overall economic efficiency.

Interestingly, there is a large and growing literature on the relationship between (income and wealth) inequality and growth, with the empirical evidence generally showing that greater inequality leads to slower growth (for a survey, see Persson and Tabellini, 1992; for some key contributions, see Meltzer and Richard, 1983; Bertola, 1991; Alesina and Rodrik, 1993). But the key linkage in these models is that greater inequality leads to more redistributive taxation in equilibrium and hence slower growth. In this sense, Buchanan's proposals would break this linkage, allowing countries with greater inequality to achieve greater growth. But whether this would be an optimal solution depends on whether there is any public good element to a more equal income distribution, and on how growth in turn affects the overall distribution of income. The latter issue is addressed in different contexts by Greenwood and Jovanovich (1991) and Aghion and Bolton (1992).

The chapter by Tommaso Padoa-Schioppa looks at the role which constitutions should play in regulating and enabling economic behaviour. As we saw in the previous chapters, there is a growing debate regarding the proper role of governments in economic policy-making, and the part constitutional provisions should play in defining this role.

Padoa-Schioppa argues that in designing economic constitutions one should recognize the role of market failures, such as the presence of pure public goods and natural monopolies. However, one should not ignore the dangers of government intervention, which arise from phenomena such as inefficient bureaucracy, and the tendency to pursue political (as opposed to social welfare) goals. Following years of greater government intervention in the postwar period, more attention is now being paid to problems of government failure, as illustrated elsewhere in this volume.

So how can one properly define the role which governments should have in economic life? Padoa-Schioppa first develops the notion of two separate 'constituencies' to which a government is related: the first, the 'political constituency', is made up of the voters; and the second is the 'economic constituency' made up of the markets. The two constituencies overlap to some extent, but the economic constituency also includes supranational elements and corporate entities which are excluded from the political constituency. One interesting development in recent years has been the growing integration of world markets, particularly financial markets, which has limited governments' room for manoeuvre. Governments are not only accountable to their political constituency, and a competent government needs to satisfy both constituencies in order to succeed. Limits to the instruments of government policy may prevent misuses and facilitate good government.

As far as the instruments of policy are concerned, Padoa-Schioppa identifies four. First, he examines the role of the 'budget', or fiscal stance. The argument here is that markets (the 'economic constituency') may not exercise sufficient control, and governments may have to be disciplined by constitutional provisions which limit budget deficits such as those incorporated in the Treaty of Maastricht. Markets may fail to exert sufficient discipline because a proper evaluation of a country's prospects depends on future political events that are often difficult to quantify. We also know from political theories of fiscal policy that bipolar political systems or coalitions of different political interests may lead to sub-optimal fiscal policy choices (see, for example, Tabellini and Alesina, 1990). Furthermore, incumbents may use budget deficits and government debt as a strategic instrument to tie the hands of future administrations (see Alesina and Perotti, 1994; Milesi-Ferretti and Spolaore, 1994).

Second, he examines the role of public debt and public ownership. In the case of debt, similar considerations apply as in the case of the budget deficit. Here Padoa-Schioppa argues that, especially where a country's public debt is held by overseas investors, tensions can emerge between the two types of constituency which could risk a crisis of confidence. To avoid the use of any debt repudiation measures, some measures of discipline should be included in an economic constitution. In the case of public ownership, Padoa-Schioppa notes that forces such as technological innovation and greater international competition are lessening the original arguments for public ownership which were based on the presence of market failure. But he also stresses that a reduction in public ownership needs to be accompanied by measures which will ensure greater efficiency.

Third, he examines the role of money and monetary policy. This is one area of debate surrounding economic constitutions which has been particularly heated in recent years. Padoa-Schioppa discusses how the German model of the central bank has influenced the evolution of other European central banks' statutes, and acted as a model for the European Central Bank in the Maastricht Treaty. The argument for delegating monetary policy to an independent central bank as a way of limiting the power of governments has been well rehearsed in the vast literature on monetary policy credibility which built on the contributions of Kydland and Prescott (1977) and Barro and Gordon (1983). More recently, the debate has shifted to the issue of whether the independent central bank should in turn be regulated, and the relationship between the preferences of the independent central bank and those of the political constituency (see, *inter alia*, Rogoff, 1985; Lohmann, 1992; Walsh, 1995; Persson and Tabellini, 1993). An important point here is also whether there are benefits to adopting an independent central bank in the presence of uncertainty regarding the preferences of the central bank or the underlying economic environment (see Lossani *et al.*, 1995; Muscatelli, 1995). In terms of Padoa-Schioppa's analysis a key issue for a future European Monetary Union is the relationship between a single European central bank and a variety of different political constituencies (see Alesina and Grilli, 1992, for an initial attempt at analysing this problem).

Fourth, Padoa-Schioppa analyses the instrument of 'command', which implies the use of coercion by the state in economic relationships. Here he notes that economic theory seems to provide little guidance in the way of general prescriptions for the limitation of the use of 'command', except in so far as it highlights some general principles. Thus, for instance, one should recognize the distortions which might arise from the interference of government in price formation. On the other hand, externalities provide a justification for government intervention such as in the protection of the environment, and governments may also have a role in protecting competition from excessive monopolistic influences.

In addition to analysing the scope of government actions which should be defined by economic constitutions, Padoa-Schioppa also highlights the important role in Europe of a two-tier economic constitution which limits the actions of national governments in several spheres of policy. However, he points out that the EU economic constitution focuses much more on the market constituency than national constitutions, which tend to be oriented towards the rights and duties of citizens. Thus, the EU economic constitution is designed to ensure that national laws are consonant with the maintenance of the 'four freedoms' (the free movement of persons, goods, services and capital within the EU). Finally, he also notes that the two-tier, national and supranational, economic constitution currently present in the EU states should be seen as the basis of a federal structure, albeit one which is built not on a multiplication of bureaucratic controls, but on the principle of subsidiarity, which ensures 'minimal government', and which is in accordance with the spirit of federalism in the tradition of Locke and Tocqueville.

The final chapter, by Anton Muscatelli, examines problems of international policy co-ordination. Some of the themes developed in the previous chapters, such as the limits which an economic constitution should place on government policy actions, are picked up again in an international context. Does the existence of macroeconomic spillover effects between countries require the imposition of some limits to individual government actions? In common with previous chapters, Muscatelli looks at the incentive structures facing governments, and at how the modelling of policy preferences leads to insights about the need to set up co-operative arrangements between countries.

The key theme underlying this chapter is whether such policy co-ordination is desirable. Most of the early literature on this subject stressed the external effects which arose from policy spillovers between countries. Co-ordination was therefore seen as a way to internalize these effects and provide a solution which was Pareto-superior to the non-co-operative one. However, more recently, and as shown in previous chapters in this volume, greater attention has been paid to divergences between social welfare objectives and the objectives of government. In the field of monetary policy, time inconsistency and credibility problems are examples of tensions which can emerge between a policy-maker and social welfare. In the case of fiscal policy, we have already come across the notion that economic constitutions may wish to impose limits on budget deficits because incumbents may use public debt strategically. If we draw the distinction between the private sector and the policy-maker in each country, the case for policy co-ordination becomes less clear, as the outcome of co-operation might be advantageous for each policy-maker, but might not improve social welfare.

Another issue confronted by Muscatelli is how such policy co-ordination might be implemented in practice, in the face of a number of difficulties, such as problems of incomplete information, the unwillingness of individual governments to abandon control over all instruments of policy, and the interdependence of macroeconomic policy instruments and microeconomic policy objectives. In some cases forms of co-operation which focus on single intermediate objectives, such as the exchange rate, have been put forward as a partial stepping-stone to full co-operation. In particular, the role of the exchange rate in monetary policy co-ordination is analysed as an example of this type of scheme.

Overall, we should note that while this series of lectures has examined a series of diverse issues, the common thread running through the volume has been the way in which the design of economic and political institutions has important effects on the workings of economic policy.

Governments, organizations and bureaucracies can be seen to react to economic incentives, and this has recently opened up a whole literature which parallels that of market failure. Government and institutional failures have forced economists to think carefully about issues of institutional design and to discuss matters which until recently were considered peripheral to economics.

References

Aghion, P. and Bolton, P. (1992). 'Distribution and growth in models with imperfect capital markets'. *European Economic Review*, 36, 603–12.

Alesina, A. (1987). 'Macroeconomic policy in a two-party system as a repeated game'. *Quarterly Journal of Economics*, 102, 651–78.

Alesina, A. (1988). 'Credibility and policy convergence in a two-party system with rational voters'. *American Economic Review*, 78, 796–805.

Alesina, A. and Grilli, V. (1992). 'The European Central Bank: reshaping monetary politics in Europe'. In M. Canzoneri, V. Grilli and P. Masson (eds), *Establishing a Central Bank. Issues in Europe and Lessons from the US*. Cambridge: Cambridge University Press.

Alesina, A. and Perotti, R. (1994). 'The political economy of budget deficits'. NBER Working Paper no. 4637.

Alesina, A. and Rodrik, D. (1993). 'Redistibutive politics and economic growth'. Mimeo, Harvard University.

Alesina, A. and Rosenthal, H. (1995). *Partisan Politics, Divided Government and the Economy*. Cambridge: Cambridge University Press.

Barro, R. and Gordon, D.B. (1983). 'Rules, discretion and reputation in a model of monetary policy'. *Journal of Monetary Economics*, 12, 101–20.

Bertola, G. (1991). 'Factor shares, saving propensities and endogenous growth'. Mimeo, Princeton University.

Greenwood, J. and Jovanovich, B. (1991). 'Financial development, growth, and the distribution of income'. *Journal of Political Economy*, 98, 1076–1107.

Kydland, F. and Prescott, E.C. (1977). 'Rules rather than discretion: the inconsistency of optimal plans'. *Journal of Political Economy*, 85, 473–91.

Laffont, J.-J. and Tirole, J. (1993). *A Theory of Incentives in Regulation and Procurement*. Cambridge, MA: MIT Press.

Lohmann, S. (1992). 'The optimal degree of commitment: credibility versus flexibility'. *American Economic Review*, 82, 273–86.

Lossani, M., Natale, P.G. and Tirelli, P. (1995). 'Incomplete information in monetary policy games: rules rather than a conservative central banker'. Mimeo, Università Cattolica, Milan.

Meltzer, A.H. and Richard, S. (1983). 'Tests of a rational theory of the size of government'. *Public Choice*, 41, 403–18.

Milesi-Ferretti, G.M. and Spolaore, E. (1994). 'How cynical can an incumbent be? Strategic policy in a model of government spending'. *Journal of Public Economics*, 55, 121–40.

Muscatelli, V.A. (1995). 'Designing monetary institutions under uncertainty: the value of the status quo'. University of Glasgow Discussion Paper.

Nordhaus, W. (1975). 'The political business cycle'. *Review of Economic Studies*, 42, 169–90.

Persson, T. and Tabellini, G. (1990). *Macroeconomic Policy, Credibility and Politics*. Chur: Harwood Academic Publishers.

Persson, T. and Tabellini, G. (1992). 'The political economy of business cycles and growth'. In A. Cukierman, C. Hercowitz, and L. Leiderman (eds), *Political Economy, Growth and Business Cycles.* Cambridge, MA: MIT Press.

Persson, T. and Tabellini, G. (1993). 'Designing institutions for monetary stability'. *Carnegie-Rochester Conference Series on Public Policy*, 39.

Rogoff, K. (1985). 'The optimal degree of commitment to an intermediate monetary target'. *Quarterly Journal of Economics*, 100, 1169–90.

Rogoff, K. and Sibert, A. (1988). 'Elections and macroeconomic policy cycles'. *Review of Economic Studies*, 55, 1–16.

Seabright, P. (1994). 'Accountability and decentralisation in government: an incomplete contracts model'. CEPR Discussion Paper, no. 899.

Tabellini, G. and Alesina, A. (1990). 'Voting on the budget deficit'. *American Economic Review*, 80, 37–49.

Walsh, C. (1995). 'Optimal contracts for central bankers'. *American Economic Review*, 85, 150–67.

2 *Anthony B. Atkinson*

The institution of an official poverty line and economic policy[1]

The title of this chapter can be read in two different ways. First, following the general theme of the 1993 Stevenson Lecture series, I am considering an official poverty line as an 'institution'. What is the role of an official poverty line in the formulation of social and economic policy? It is in this sense a case study of the role of national targets in the conduct of policy. In the classic theory of economic policy set out by Tinbergen (1952; 1954), is the elimination of poverty a fixed or a flexible target? If the target is a flexible one, how do we trade reductions in poverty against gains in other objectives? Or, as viewed in recent theories of economic policy, is the setting of a poverty goal a way of precommitting future policy, and, if so, why should either politicians or citizens wish to commit themselves in such a way?

Second, the word institution can be read as deriving from an active verb, for the setting in place of a poverty line, and the second aspect I want to address is whether or not the United Kingdom should set in place an official poverty line. What can we learn from the analysis of the poverty line as an institution that is relevant for social policy in the UK? Would it be desirable for the government to adopt an explicit poverty target? The answer will clearly depend in part on judgements of value, but we may at least be able to clarify some of the arguments.

The fact that the UK does not have an official poverty line is remarkable in view of the pioneering contributions of UK social scientists to the study of poverty and to the predominance of poverty among the concerns that led to its social security system. The next section of this paper begins by tracing briefly the history of official attitudes to poverty measurement in the UK and the latent ambiguities. Then, a contrast is drawn with the approach adopted in the European Community. The best-known experience with an official poverty line is, however, that of the United States, and the section concludes by focusing on that experience. A great deal has been written about the US poverty line, but it is striking how little discussion there appears to have been as to the consequences of having such an official line. The functions or dysfunctions of this social institution seem to have been surprisingly little investigated.

The third section of the paper explores the role of such a poverty target, setting it in the context of the formulation of economic policy. To this end, I first have recourse to what I learned as the *theory of economic policy*: Tinbergen's theory of objectives and constraints. I then turn to what may be called the *new* theory of policy which has recently been influential in macroeconomics. This analysis forms the basis for the discussion in the fourth section of the question as to whether it would be desirable to institute an official poverty line in Britain.

Reference has been made to the UK, the European Community and the USA, and I should make clear at the outset that I am considering poverty in rich countries. This is very different from poverty on a world scale. The US official poverty line is more than six times the average per capita income of India.[2] It could well be argued that poverty in Africa and Asia is so important as to preclude any consideration of the deprived within OECD countries. While it is my own personal judgement that world poverty has priority, I do not accept that this leaves no room for consideration of poverty in Britain. Even if all ships in reach of the *Titanic* had an overriding obligation to steam to its rescue, this does not mean that they should not have taken steps to protect their steerage passengers from exposure.

Poverty lines

History of poverty lines in the UK

The history of poverty lines in the United Kingdom is a history of ambiguity, particularly that concerning the relation between poverty standards and the scales of benefit provided under National Insurance or Income Support.

The two – poverty standards and benefit scales – have grown up together. The studies of subsistence needs by Rowntree at the turn of the century preceded by a few years the introduction of state old age pensions in 1908. The first major step towards the creation of modern social assistance, with the establishment of the Unemployment Assistance Board in 1934, was almost simultaneous with Rowntree's work on *The Human Needs of Labour* (1937). There was, however, little direct relation between poverty standards and benefit scales. According to Lynes (1977, p. 43), the Unemployment Assistance Board paid little attention to the calculations of subsistence needs when setting scale rates.

It was in the Beveridge Report of 1942 that the two came closest to being joined. Rowntree served as a member of the sub-committee which advised on benefit scales, and Beveridge (1942, p. 14) stated that 'social insurance should aim at guaranteeing the minimum income needed for subsistence'. On the other hand, this was not the only consideration influencing the determination of benefit scales. Beveridge was throughout mindful of the cost of his proposals, and the Committee was concerned with the relation between benefits and the net earnings of those in work. The message that the Report tried to convey was that the national minimum could be achieved without violating the constraints of cost or those arising from incentive considerations. It is, however, open to question how far this was achieved by adjusting the benefit scales to the affordable resources rather than vice versa. Veit Wilson (1989, p. 85), on the basis of his research on the Beveridge Committee papers, argues that 'the driving forces were the need . . . to keep costs largely within what could be taxed by horizontal redistribution by national insurance within the working class, and not to set scales which, it was believed, would remove the incentives to earn'. For all its stirring prose, the Beveridge Report is an essentially ambiguous document when it comes to the relation between objectives and constraints.

In any case, as is well known, the postwar legislation setting in place a national minimum rejected Beveridge's recommendation that the minimum should be guaranteed by social insurance. Instead it was National Assistance, the means-tested scheme, which played this role. And it was to National Assistance that social investigators in the postwar period looked when seeking a standard by which to judge the effectiveness of the welfare state. In *The Poor and the Poorest*, Abel-Smith and Townsend (1965, p. 17) took the National Assistance scale as their starting point, saying that: 'Whatever may be said about the adequacy of the National Assistance Board level of living as a just or publicly approved measure of "poverty", it has at least the advantage of being in a sense the "official" operational definition of the minimum level of living at any particular time'. Later authors followed their lead in using as a 'performance standard' the level of National Assistance, by then renamed Supplementary Benefit, and now called Income Support. The success of income maintenance policy was being judged in terms of its effectiveness in securing a national minimum at the level chosen by the government itself. This in turn was the standard applied for a number of years in the official studies of *Low Income Families*, which examined how many people had incomes below the Supplementary Benefit scale or within a certain percentage of that scale (Department of Health and Social Security, 1988).

There was, however, no official poverty line, and no one suggested that the Income Support scale was appropriate for this purpose. As reiterated by successive government spokesmen, both Labour and Conservative, any improvement in Income Support would, on this basis, lead to an *increase* in measured poverty.[3] The position was made quite clear by Mrs Thatcher in July 1983, when she said at Prime Minister's Questions that: 'There is no definition of the poverty line – [Hon Members: "Oh."] – and there never has been under any Government' (*Hansard*, 14 July 1983, vol. 45, col. 1008). The 1985 Green Paper on the *Reform of Social Security* stated that 'there is now no universally agreed standard of poverty' (Department of Health and Social Security, 1985, p. 12), still less one that had official approval. In May 1989, the then Secretary of State for Social Security, John Moore, went further and attacked the whole idea that there might be poverty in the UK. In a speech called 'The End of the Line for Poverty', he argued that poverty had been abolished, and that it therefore made no sense to use the word.

The European Community poverty line

The Conservative government was particularly concerned to attack the notion of poverty which had been adopted by the European Community. Whereas the UK government has no official poverty line, the European Commission has established such a criterion, stating that: 'The poor shall be taken to mean persons, families and groups of persons whose resources (material, cultural and social) are so limited as to exclude them from the minimum acceptable way of life in the Member States in which they live' (Commission of the European Communities, 1989, p. 9). This is the definition contained in a decision of the Council of Ministers when approving the first Community Action Programme to Combat Poverty. In its evaluation of the Programme, the Commission took as the concrete implementation of this definition a poverty standard of 50 per cent of the average disposable income per equivalent adult in the country in question. Eurostat publishes official statistics showing on this basis a league table for poverty in the member states.

There is, therefore, an official European Community poverty line. And there are other countries which have official poverty lines, notably the United States, where the official standard has played a major role. As it has been put by Lampman (1974, p. 67), 'no other nation had set out a performance goal so explicit with regard to the "poor"'.

Official poverty lines: the experience of the United States

The United States poverty line dates back to the War on Poverty declared by President Johnson in 1964. The Council of Economic Advisors Report in that year defined the poverty line as $3,000 a year for a family and $1,500 for a single person. This was based on research by Orshansky (1965), who subsequently produced a refined, more differentiated, poverty line. This line was adopted by the Office of Economic Opportunity as 'a working definition of poverty for statistical, planning and budget purposes' in May 1965 (Fisher, 1992, p. 9). In August 1969, the Bureau of the Budget designated a modified version of the line as the federal government's official statistical definition of poverty.

Today, the official poverty line is still going strong. It has been modified in certain respects and has of course been adjusted over time. The official method of adjustment is in line with the Consumer Price Index, which means that it fell as a proportion of median income at the time when the latter was rising in real terms. In 1963 the poverty line for a family of four was 50.1 per cent of median family income – or essentially the European half of average income – but by 1973 it had fallen to 37.7 per cent. Since then it has varied little in relative terms (Weinberg and Lamas, 1991). In 1990 the poverty line for a family of four was $13,359 a year, or £165 a week, and 13.5 per cent of the US population was living below this level.

The US official poverty line plays a role in the allocation of federal funds and in the determination of individual benefits. For example, the National School Lunch Program and the School Breakfast Program provide free meals to those families with incomes below 130 per cent of the official poverty line (Committee on Ways and Means, 1992, p. 1683); under the Special Supplemental Food Program for Women, Infants and Children (WIC), states must set an eligibility level between 100 and 185 per cent of the official poverty line (*ibid.*, p. 1687).

At the same time, there is an important separation between the poverty line and the determination of benefits. There is no guarantee that the cash transfer programmes will bring people up to the official poverty level. In January 1992, under the Aid to Families with Dependent

Children (AFDC) programme, the maximum benefit, including food stamps, in the median state – since it varies by state – for a single-parent family of three was only 72 per cent of the poverty threshold (Committee on Ways and Means, 1992, p. 637). In 1988, the total benefit from AFDC and food stamps combined was below 60 per cent of the poverty level in 16 states and below 75 per cent in 39 states (Center on Social Welfare Policy and Law, 1988). For the elderly, the level of the Supplemental Security Income (SSI) plus social security and food stamps was 86.2 per cent of the poverty threshold for a single person (Committee on Ways and Means, 1992, p. 798).

The official poverty line is much discussed in the USA. This applies to the implications of the findings from studies of poverty, where the failure to eliminate poverty has been a recurring concern. It applies to the design of the poverty standard, where from the outset it has been the subject of critical comment (for example, Friedman, 1965); and in 1992 a National Academy of Sciences expert panel was charged with reviewing the poverty standard.

What seems to have been much less discussed, rather surprisingly, is the role played by the existence of an official poverty line. What difference does it make to have an official standard? Did it have any significance that it has been designated officially in this way, rather than being simply the product of academic research?

Among the relatively small number of people who have commented on this issue, the general opinion seems to be that it *does* make a difference. According to Tobin (1970, p. 83):

> The Federal 'war on poverty', whatever else it has accomplished, has established an official measure of the prevalence of poverty in the United States. Adoption of a specific quantitative measure, however arbitrary and debatable, will have durable and far-reaching political consequences. Administrations will be judged by their success or failure in reducing the officially measured prevalence of poverty. So long as any families are found below the official poverty line, no politician will be able to claim victory in the war on poverty or ignore the repeated solemn acknowledgements of society's obligations to its poorer members.

This assessment was quoted approvingly nearly two decades later by Haveman (1987, p. 55) in his evaluation of the impact of social science research, where he says that 'adoption of the "Orshansky line" as the official measure of poverty represents an important example of the effect of research, combined with a certain amount of political compromise, on policy-making'.

What is less evident is how exactly it makes a difference. This question is now examined from a theoretical point of view, starting from the theory of economic policy.

A poverty line and the theory of economic policy

The theory of economic policy

The classic theory of economic policy is that associated with Tinbergen, and, although this theory may today be regarded as rather old-fashioned when compared with the modern game-theoretic treatment of policy-making, I believe that it can make a valuable contribution to clarifying our thinking.

To begin with, it is central to Tinbergen's approach that the process of policy-making be viewed as an integrated whole. As described in his essay *On the Theory of Economic Policy*:

> It has taken a considerably long time before even economists looked at economic policy as a *coherent entity*. In most textbooks on economics or on economic policy separate components such as trade policy, agricultural policy, credit policy, wage policy are considered without much attention to their interdependence and the targets and instruments of each of these components are often considered in isolation, this general coherence being neglected. Yet this interdependence is a reality and therefore the unit to be considered is the totality of all measures. (Tinbergen, 1952, p. 68; emphasis in original)[4]

In the present context, this means that we cannot consider anti-poverty policy in isolation from other objectives. This is perhaps self-evident in an intellectual sense. The scope for financing income maintenance depends on macroeconomic policy choices, on levels of government spending, and on rates of inflation. The use of transfer payments, or other instruments of anti-poverty policy, such as education and training or health care, in turn have implications for economic policy. Social and economic policy are interdependent.

This may appear obvious, but it remains the case that social policy is often placed in a separate compartment. Economic policy tends to have first claim on our attention, with social policy accommodating to the results. This is alarming not just because of the interdependence, but also because it appears that undue faith is placed in the efficacy of social policy to solve the distributional problems generated by macroeconomic policy.

Table 2.1 Indicators of performance

	Inflation 1979–90 (% per year)	Unemployment 1980–90 (%)	Poverty 1985 (%)
Netherlands	2.8	9.5	11.4
West Germany	2.9	5.8	9.9
Belgium	4.7	10.4	5.9
France	6.9	9.0	15.7
United Kingdom	7.5	9.7	18.2
Spain	9.9	17.4	18.9
Italy	10.6	9.5	15.5

Sources: Inflation: average annual percentage rate of change of consumer price indices, from OECD (1992, Table 8.11). Unemployment: standardized unemployment rates as percentage of total labour force, from OECD (1992, Table 2.20). Poverty: rates for persons from Eurostat (1990, Table 1).

There is, therefore, a lot to be said for a unified approach to policy-making. This means in turn that, while we are used to thinking about targets for inflation, unemployment and growth, now in the same table we have to record performance in avoiding poverty. To make this concrete, let us take the two macro-indicators which receive most attention: inflation and unemployment. The performance of seven European countries, averaged over the 1980s, is shown in Table 2.1. (The degree of comparability of the data is not considered here.)

The countries are listed in Table 2.1 in order of their inflation performance, with the lowest annual inflation rate at the top, and this is rather different from their ranking according to standardized unemployment rates, where the Netherlands and Belgium do less well and Italy performs better. Alongside these macroeconomic indicators is shown in the third column the poverty rate in 1985, measured according to the poverty standard set by the European Commission as half of average national income. The order of the first three is now reversed, compared to the inflation ranking, with Belgium coming top (i.e. with lowest poverty) and Italy performing better. It is, however, striking that the ranking of countries by poverty rates is closer to that by inflation rates than that by unemployment rates. This is surprising since we might expect unemployment to be a proxy indicator of poverty; the explanation must be that the consequences of unemployment depend, among other things, on the social protection in force.

Sometimes journalists form a so-called 'misery index' of economic performance, by adding the inflation and unemployment rates. We could go further and sum the three indicators, which gives a ranking with West Germany top, followed by Belgium and Netherlands, then France, with the UK and Italy virtually the same, and Spain bottom. Such a calculation, however, immediately leads us to ask what *is* the trade-off in our objective functions between these different indicators. Do we in fact weight them equally? The sheer crudity of such a numerical exercise makes clear that there are a number of welfare economic questions that need to be answered. We need to consider more deeply the precise nature of social objectives.

Objectives and constraints

The first question concerns the distinction, drawn by Tinbergen, between *fixed* and *flexible* targets. The former specifies policy objectives in absolute terms. Policy must ensure that the balance of payments is in equilibrium or that the borrowing requirement does not exceed *x* per cent of national income. These are fixed targets. In contrast, a flexible target is one that indicates the direction in which we are aiming but where it is recognized that there may be limits to the extent that it can be attained. We may then have to trade gains in one direction against losses in another, the form of the trade-off being indicated by the social welfare function.

In the case of poverty, we could require that there be a fixed target of eliminating all poverty as measured by an agreed standard. The abolition of want was the announced intention of the Beveridge Report of 1942. This, however, was misleading in that we have seen that behind the report lay a balancing of the benefit levels with considerations of cost and incentive constraints. Beveridge claimed that the level of the subsistence standard determined the level of social insurance benefits, but in reality the choice of target was influenced by what was feasible. And in a European context, the poverty target, as defined by the European Commission, has not typically been attained.

It does not in fact seem reasonable to see the elimination of poverty as a fixed target. Rather, it is a flexible target, the attainment of which is limited on account of the constraints faced by the government. These constraints in turn are unlikely to be absolute, but rather to involve a trade-off between different objectives. The government may in this

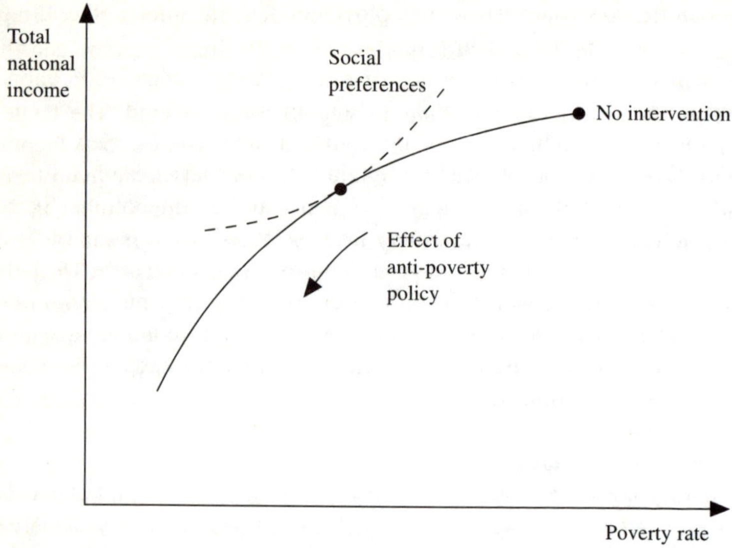

Figure 2.1 Policy trade-off between poverty rate and total national income

case set the transfer payments at a level below the poverty line, because to raise them further would reduce other indicators of performance to a level it considers unsatisfactory. As it was put by the UK government:

> Even if it were possible to arrive at some general consensus on a minimum acceptable income, this would not necessarily provide a determination of the level of benefits to be paid . . . rates are not set in isolation: the Government gives due regard to the relationship between benefit levels and the rewards available to those in work, and to the total resources available for public spending. (Department of Social Security, 1989, p. 5)

To make the discussion more concrete, let us suppose that anti-poverty policy reduces poverty, but at the cost of higher taxes which have an adverse effect on total national income. I should emphasize that in my view the disincentive effects of taxation have been greatly exaggerated and that the existence of transfers may have a positive impact on total income. However, for the present argument, let us suppose that there is an efficiency–equity trade-off as shown in Figure 2.1. We then have to consider the trade-off on the preference side between total income and poverty reduction. How much aggregate income are we willing to give up in order to reduce poverty from 15 per cent to 10 per cent? There is, on the Tinbergen approach, a social welfare function defined over the level of the national income and the level of poverty.

This framework allows certain aspects to be considered. The United Kingdom, for example, in the 1980s witnessed a rise in total income and a rise in poverty. In terms of Figure 2.1, there was a move upwards and to the right. If all that had happened was an improvement in the possibility set, then we should have expected an improvement on both fronts (assuming that both objectives are normal goods), so that the move would have been upwards and to the left. On this interpretation, we have therefore either had a shift in social preferences against poverty reduction (a change in the shape of the indifference curves) or a change in the shape of the feasibility frontier, with poverty reduction becoming more expensive.

This formulation forces us in turn to think more deeply about the nature of the poverty objective. Here standard welfare economics turns out not to be very helpful. Concern with poverty does not follow, at least directly, from standard formulations of policy objectives. Viewed from the standpoint of welfare economics, maximization of a Bergson–Samuelson social welfare function does not of itself imply that weight is attached to ensuring a national minimum. It is not a feature of a utilitarian objective, or of more general functions taking individual welfares as their arguments, that special significance is attached to any particular level of income or welfare. The weighting of marginal increases in income implied by the social welfare function may, of course, mean that priority is given to transfers to those at the bottom of the income scale. The extreme case of priority is that of the Rawlsian difference principle under which the welfare of the least advantaged is maximized. But this is not the same as concern with a poverty standard. This may be seen from the fact that it is conceivable that poverty is zero (for example, no one has an income below half the mean), so that total income is the sole concern, whereas on a Rawlsian criterion it is the lowest income that remains the objective.

Nor can a justification for a safety net be derived directly from theories of the state that reject the idea of a social welfare function and see redistribution as only justified by appeal to individual preferences. This refers to the theory of Pareto-improving transfers, where they are justified on the grounds that those financing the transfer are concerned about the welfare of the recipients. Wiseman (1991, p. 55), for example, identifies 'welfare' 'with the *existence of caring feelings* [such that] individual citizens believe that a reduction in their own material well-being is desirable if accompanied by particular improvements in the well-being of other citizens' (emphasis in original). But, as he goes on to emphasize, 'the form and extent of such caring feelings is not a given, any more than is their taste for apples' (*ibid.*). Individuals may desire to see transfers made to reduce poverty, but their preferences could in theory lead to any form of redistribution.

These observations suggest that an explicit justification for a poverty standard must be sought outside standard welfare economics. The social preferences posited in Figure 2.1 cannot be regarded simply as a reduced form of a social welfare maximization problem or as reflecting some specific individual preferences.

The new theory of economic policy

So far I have tried to relate the official poverty objective to the old-fashioned theory of economic policy. More recently, the theory has taken a different course. As described by Persson and Tabellini (1990, p. ix):

> In contrast to most earlier work, the new work treats the government as responding to incentives, not to orders . . . It specifies a government objective and views equilibrium policy as the optimal choice given the objective and various constraints. This approach leads to positive models of economic policy in alternative institutional environments.

This resembles, in a public finance context, the approach adopted by public choice theorists, associated particularly with Buchanan and Tullock.

This approach leads us to ask what role would be played in the positive analysis of policy formation by an official poverty target. Why should any government accept such a target and what would be its implications? Would the existence of an official poverty line make any difference?

Economists often pride themselves on not being interested in rhetoric. It is not relevant what people *say* they do; all that matters is what they actually *do*. We can infer from their actions what are their preferences, and listening to what they state to be their objectives makes no difference to our understanding. On the other hand, many non-economists believe that stated objectives are relevant, and that it may be useful to distinguish between these and the preferences which appear to underlie the observed policy choices.

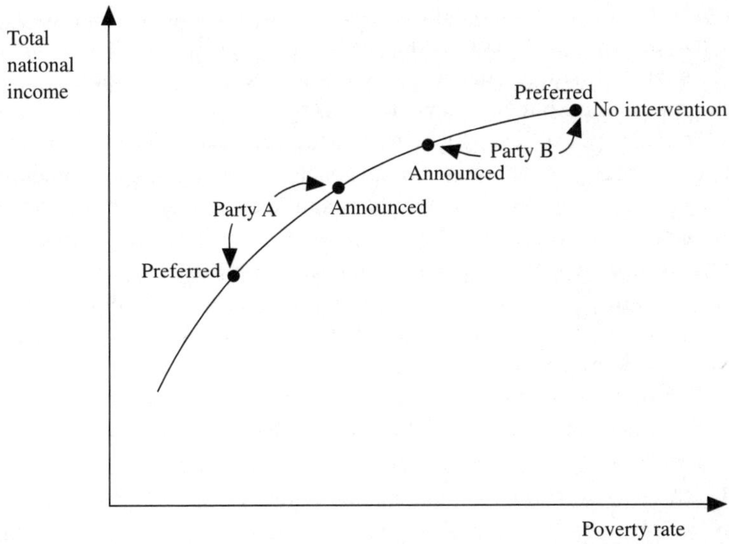

Figure 2.2 Choice of party platform

Why should this be? Why should the existence of an explicit target lead to a different outcome from the situation where the government simply acts as though there were a target? The answer clearly depends on the model of behaviour supposed to apply to the government. Many such models have been proposed and there is little consensus as to the most appropriate. Moreover, the most appropriate model is likely to vary over space and time. Here I take a starkly simplified approach. Suppose that there are two political parties concerned with being in power, and with achieving their interests, which are different for the two parties. (The model is based on that of two-party competition described by Alesina, 1988.) In order to dramatize the situation, suppose that one party, A, has a strong preference for an extensive anti-poverty programme, as shown in Figure 2.2, and that the other, B, is only concerned with total income. Suppose, furthermore, that policy can be represented along the single dimension of the level of anti-poverty policy, which is a big 'if' and the Achilles' heel of this approach. Voters have preferences over different levels of transfers and the implied tax rate. As far as the parties are concerned, the outcome of the election is uncertain, and each acts as though the probability of winning is a function of the chosen policies of the two parties. The form of the function is assumed to be such that a party can increase its chance of election by converging towards the policy of its opponent.[5]

In such a situation, one would expect to find a convergence of political programmes, but not complete convergence.[6] Neither political party will pursue the policy which maximizes its own objective function, since it recognizes that some compromise will increase the probability of winning the election. On the other hand, the convergence is less than complete because parties attach some weight to their own objectives. Party B will propose a benefit level less than that of party A even though closing the gap would raise its probability of winning, since it would reduce the value of winning (being committed to a higher benefit level than it believes desirable).

What role would a poverty target play in these circumstances? Why should either party espouse such a target? It may appear obvious why party A would establish such a target, since it is concerned about poverty, but why should party B accept an official poverty objective, when it is opposed to anti-poverty policy?

One answer lies in the kind of argument which macroeconomists have been making in recent years: that there may be problems with the time consistency of policy. The description of the electoral competition assumed that political parties are precommitted to a policy, whereas once elected they may in fact decide to follow their own preferences and not the policy on which they campaigned. If party B wins, it could then set transfers to zero, even if it had promised to maintain a certain level. As argued by Alesina (1988), if voters are rational, they take this into account, and in the limit they disregard the announced platforms. The outcome simply depends on the preferred choices of the political parties.

In such a situation, however, it may be in the interest of political parties to try and persuade voters that they will not act purely in their own interests once elected. In particular, party B may want to precommit itself to spend more than zero. The adoption of an official poverty line may represent a precommitment of this type. By announcing this target, party B may bind itself not to cut benefits, and the sophisticated electorate will therefore find it more acceptable, since it will remain closer to its campaign promises. This provides one argument why a party on the right would find it in its own interests to adopt a poverty target. Paradoxically, it is the party not concerned about poverty which adopts the poverty target.

What about party A? Party A finds it in its own interest to precommit itself not to spend as much on benefits as it would like, and here the announcement of a poverty target may worsen rather than improve its prospects. Such a precommitment would simply reinforce voters' suspicions that party A would be profligate with their money. On the other hand, the policy choice of the opposition is closer to its own preference. The adoption of a commitment may in fact make both parties better off.

Should the UK have an official poverty line?

So far we have been engaged in a positive analysis of the determination of policy. What normative conclusions can be drawn about the desirability of a precommitment to an official poverty target?

In the model of party platform choice, there is no guarantee that the electoral equilibrium without precommitment is Pareto-efficient. There may well be a range of policies, lying between the extreme 'party preferred' choices, which are considered better by all members of the electorate. The existence of the precommitment means that they are offered a different set of policies, and a choice between the 'announced' policies in Figure 2.2 may be seen as better than a choice between the more extreme policies. Voters may be better off – although there is no presumption that this is the case.

It is also possible that voters, as well as politicians, can benefit from being tied like Ulysses to the mast. Suppose that people have different levels of preference: higher and lower selves. One's higher self may exhibit concern for the poor, whereas one's lower self may consult only private interest. In one's higher thinking, one may be persuaded by arguments that policy should be judged from behind a veil of ignorance, but when it comes to an election one may only take account of self-interest. Recognizing our weakness, we may in this situation prefer, according to our higher selves, to be precommitted to a policy which takes account of poverty. Put another way, the existence of an official poverty line may limit the range of policies which are put to the electorate. Voters are not exposed to temptation.

Turning to less formal, but possibly richer, models of political behaviour, we may relate the role of the poverty line to that of performance standards in government and the pressures for greater accountability, as in the Citizen's Charter. In this regard, the existence of an official poverty line would serve to increase public awareness. The press and media would find such a poverty standard simple to describe, and there would be clear topical interest in the performance according to this target. In the United States, newspapers know when the annual poverty count is to be released and line up academic commentators. The regular performance test would contribute to keeping the issue on the public agenda and to deepening public debate. In this connection, we should note the importance attributed by Drèze and Sen (1989) to the role played by the press and media in the avoidance of famine in countries such as India.

Could we, however, agree on an official poverty standard? As earlier noted, the formulation of the poverty target raises questions. It does not fit into traditional welfare economics, and it may be difficult to specify the trade-off with other objectives. It may also be difficult to specify in its own terms. There are many dimensions to a poverty standard and much scope for differences of opinion. There is the level of the poverty line, and the method of uprating over time (reference was made earlier to the US practice of indexation in line with prices, which in the UK would have had quite different consequences from indexation with real incomes). There is the definition of income when measuring poverty, a subject which has attracted considerable attention in the US particularly with regard to the inclusion or exclusion of benefits in kind. There is the time period over which income is measured. A person may be poor this month, but comfortably out of poverty next month and on average over the year is not in poverty at all. There is the definition of the unit of analysis, where it may make quite a difference whether we treat a household as a whole, or consider the position of families or individuals.

All of these pose formidable problems, and it is far from clear that we could agree on a national target. At the same time, there are two considerations which make the task of agreement easier. First, there is an important difference between agreeing on a criterion according to which benefits are to be paid and agreeing on a definition for purely statistical purposes. If it is an aggregate poverty statistic that is the end product, then a certain amount of rough justice may be acceptable. We do not have to worry about the administrative apparatus for determining benefit eligibility.

Second, it may be possible to identify common ground if not complete agreement. People may prefer an imperfect measure to one that matches their ideal in all respects. They may agree that the poverty line for a single person should be at least £*x* a week, even if they do not agree how much higher it should be. We may, therefore, set an official standard which the majority regard as too low, but which very few regard as too high. In his assessment of the US poverty line, Kershaw

(1970, p. 13) says that 'it works' because: 'Although the definition undoubtedly classifies some poor people as nonpoor, it classifies very few nonpoor as poor. Objections are raised from time to time, but rarely does anyone assert that . . . any appreciable number of those counted as poor are really nonpoor'.

Conclusions

The institution of an official poverty line has received remarkably little attention. Few people appear to have asked whether it makes a difference to have such a target. Little account has been taken of the role of announced objectives in influencing the behaviour of policy-makers.

There are in fact a number of ways in which the existence of an official objective could affect the direction of policy. I have only considered some of these, and have concentrated primarily on the integration of the poverty objective into the theory of economic policy which has been more commonly concerned with macroeconomic variables. This integration seems to me important in view of the need to confront economic policy with its social consequences, to allow a unified assessment of national performance. Even though there are undoubtedly differences of opinion, a limited degree of agreement appears possible, and could increase the influence of the citizens over the government.

My aim in this chapter has been to raise a question which has been too little discussed. Whether or not we should in fact adopt an official poverty standard is a matter on which we all have to form our own personal view. My own view favours the adoption of an official poverty line in the UK and the cementing of that which has begun to play a role in the European Community. To quote Haveman (1993, p. 27) in the USA, the panel reviewing the poverty line 'has the mandate, and hence a great opportunity, to change an important element of how we as a nation view ourselves. The definition of poverty . . . that is officially adopted will be a crucial statistical indicator of national performance. Like the unemployment rate, the poverty measure embodies a national goal'. In Europe, we need such a Community goal to set alongside the more narrowly economic objectives of closer integration.

Notes

1 This chapter is a revised version of a paper presented as one of the 1993 series of Stevenson Lectures in Citizenship at the University of Glasgow.

I am grateful to Robert Haveman for his most helpful comments on the first draft.

2 In 1988, the poverty threshold for an unrelated individual in the USA was some $6,000 a year, whereas US GNP per capita was some $20,000. The purchasing power estimates of the World Bank show that GDP per capita in India was some 4.5 per cent of that in the USA (World Bank, 1990, Table 30).

3 This was one of the main reasons why the *Low Income Families* study was replaced by the *Households Below Average Income* reports.

4 The situation prior to Tinbergen's *Theory of Economic Policy* has been described by Hansen (1974, pp. xvi–xvii):

> the tradition had always been to consider various types of economic policy separately and discuss them in relation to particular targets. Fiscal policy, monetary policy, foreign exchange policy, labour market policy, etc., fell apart into so many different policies; policy targets related to the price level, employment, the balance of payments, income distribution, etc., were often dealt with in isolation.

5 Denoting the policy of party A by X_A, and that of party B by X_B, in the region where $X_A > X_B$, the probability of election of party A is a declining function of X_A and the probability of election of party B is an increasing function of X_B.

6 Denoting by $p(X_A, X_B)$ the probability of election of party A, and by $U_A(X)$ the utility of party A if policy X is followed, then if the party maximizes

$$pU_A(X_A) + (1 - p)U_A(X_B)$$

then the derivative with respect to X_A is

$$pU'_A(X_A) - [U_A(X_A) - U_A(X_B)]\{-\partial p/\partial X_A\}$$

It follows that the policy chosen lies between X_B and that which maximizes $U_A(X)$.

References

Abel-Smith, B. and Townsend, P. (1965). *The Poor and the Poorest*. London: Bell.

Alesina, A. (1988). 'Credibility and policy convergence in a two-party system with rational voters'. *American Economic Review*, 78, 796–805.

Beveridge, Lord (1942). *Social Insurance and Allied Services*, Cmd. 6404. London: HMSO.

Center on Social Welfare Policy and Law (1988). *Analysis of 1988 Benefit Levels in the Program of Aid to Families with Dependent Children*. New York.

Commission of the European Communities (1989). *Interim Report on a Specific Community Action Programme to Combat Poverty*. Brussels.

Committee on Ways and Means, US House of Representatives (1992). *Green Book*. Washington, DC: US Government Printing Office.

Department of Health and Social Security (1985). *Reform of Social Security*, Cmnd. 9517. London: HMSO.

Department of Health and Social Security (1988). *Low Income Families 1985*. London: Department of Health and Social Security.

Department of Social Security (1989). 'Benefit levels and minimum income'. In House of Commons Social Services Committee, *Minimum Income*. London: HMSO.

Drèze, J.P. and Sen, A.K. (1989). *Hunger and Public Action*. Oxford: Clarendon Press.

Eurostat (1990). *Inequality and Poverty in Europe (1980–1985)*, Rapid Reports, 1990: 7. Luxembourg: Eurostat.

Fisher, G.M. (1992). 'The development and history of the poverty thresholds'. *Social Security Bulletin*, 55: 4, 3–46.

Friedman, R.D. (1965). *Poverty – Definition and Perspective*. Washington, DC: American Enterprise Institute.

Hansen, B. (1974). 'Introduction'. In W. Sellekaerts (ed.), *Econometrics and Economic Theory, Essays in Honour of Jan Tinbergen*. London: Macmillan.

Haveman, R.H. (1987). *Poverty Policy and Poverty Research*. Madison: University of Wisconsin Press.

Haveman, R.H. (1993). 'Who are the nation's "truly poor"?'. *The Brookings Review*, Winter, 24–27.

Kershaw, J.A. (1970). *Government against Poverty*. Washington, DC: Brookings Institution.

Lampman, R.J. (1974). 'What does it do for the poor? A new test for national policy'. *Public Interest*, 34, 66–82.

Lynes, T. (1977). 'The making of the unemployment assistance scale'. In Department of Health and Social Security, *Low Incomes*, Supplementary Benefits Administration Papers 6. London: HMSO, Appendix 1.

OECD (1992). *Historical Statistics 1960–1990*. Paris: OECD.

Orshansky, M. (1965). 'Counting the poor: another look at the poverty profile'. *Social Security Bulletin*, 28, 3–29.

Persson, T. and Tabellini, G. (1990). *Macroeconomic Policy, Credibility and Politics*. Chur: Harwood Academic Publishers.

Rowntree, B.S. (1937). *The Human Needs of Labour*. London: Longmans.

Tinbergen, J. (1952). *On the Theory of Economic Policy*. Amsterdam: North-Holland.

Tinbergen, J. (1954). *Centralization and Decentralization in Economic Policy*. Amsterdam: North-Holland.

Tobin, J. (1970). 'Raising the incomes of the poor'. In K. Gordon (ed.), *Agenda for the Nation*. Washington, DC: Brookings Institution.

Veit Wilson, J. (1989). Memorandum. In House of Commons Social Services Committee, *Minimum Income*. London: HMSO.

Weinberg, D. and Lamas, E.J. (1991). *The History and Current Issues of U.S. Poverty Measurement*. Washington, DC: US Bureau of the Census.

Wiseman, J. (1991). 'The welfare state: a public choice perspective'. In T. Wilson and D. Wilson (eds), *The State and Social Welfare*. London: Longman.

World Bank (1990). *World Development Report 1990*. Oxford: Oxford University Press.

3 *Alberto Alesina*

Elections and the economy: the case of the United States, with some lessons for Europe

The facts

General elections and economic conditions influence each other in many ways. On the one hand, elections are won or lost because of the state of the economy. On the other hand, economic policies reflect partisan influences and politicians choose policies with an eye on voters' preferences.

A large literature has studied these issues, particularly for the case of the United States.[1] This research has uncovered and attempted to explain several observations which characterize the US political economy of this century, or, at least, of the period since the Second World War.

1) Government is often divided; that is, the party holding the presidency does not have a majority in the House and in the Senate. Table 3.1 shows that in the postwar period a majority of elections have resulted in divided government. Furthermore, the last half of a century is *not* an exception: divided government was common even in the last century.

2) The party holding the White House loses plurality and seats in mid-term congressional elections; this is the so called 'mid-term cycle' in which the US electorate always turns against the president's party. Figure 3.1 exhibits this very strong regulator for the period 1918 to 1992.

3) Presidential elections are strongly influenced by the state of the economy; in particular, incumbents are more likely to be reappointed if the rate of GNP growth in the election year is high. The term 'incumbent' is used to indicate either the person or the party in office.

4) The rate of GNP growth in election years is not significantly higher than in non-election years.

Table 3.2 highlights the last two observations. The rate of growth is much higher than average when incumbents are reappointed, while it is below average when they are not. The latter observation emerges even

Table 3.1 Control of national institutions in the United States, 1832–1992

	Number of national elections resulting in unified government	divided government
1832–1992	50	30
1832–1900	20	14
1900–1952	22	4
1952–1992	8	12

Source: Fiorina (1991), updated by the author

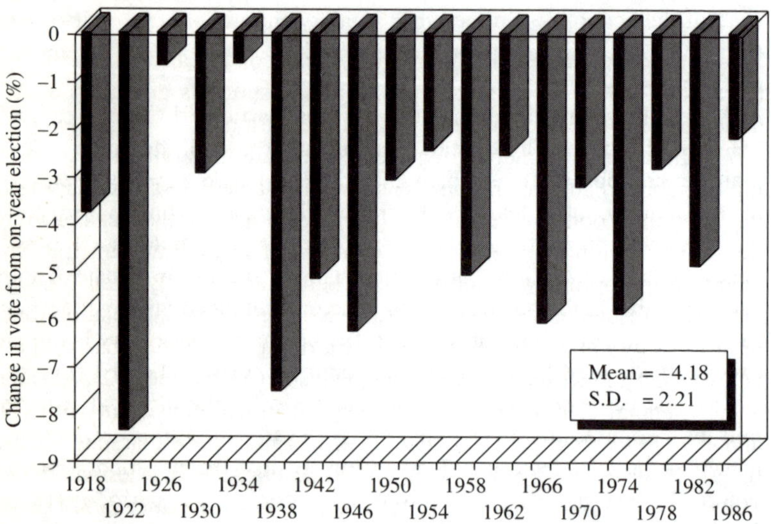

Figure 3.1 The mid-term cycle: the president's party's share of House vote

more clearly when 1976 is excluded: that particular election was largely driven by Watergate. The last two rows indicate that the average rate of growth of GNP in election years is slightly *below* the sample average.

5) Congressional elections are less sensitive to the state of the economy than presidential elections.

6) The rate of GNP growth is high after a presidential victory of the Democratic Party, and low after a victory of the Republican Party.

Table 3.2 GNP growth and elections: sample, 1948–91

	Average GNP growth
(1) Presidential election years with incumbent party reappointed	4.7
(2) President election years with incumbent party not reappointed	3.0
(3) Same as (2), excluding 1976	2.5
(4) Average of any presidential election year	3.1
(5) Sample average	3.7

Source: Economic Report of the President (1992)

This difference reaches a maximum in the second year of the term. In the second halves of the two types of administrations growth is about the same. Table 3.3 documents these observations.

7) Inflation is higher during Democratic administrations than during Republican administrations, as shown in Table 3.4. The collapse of the Bretton Woods system in 1971 generates a natural 'break' in the time series of inflation rates. Thus, comparisons across administrations are more appropriate within the periods before and after Bretton Woods.

Several researchers have studied these observations in isolation, one or at most two at a time. For instance Fiorina (1988; 1991) has studied (1); Alesina and Rosenthal (1989) and Erikson (1988) study (2); Alesina and Rosenthal (1996) provide a theoretical model consistent with (1) and (2). Kramer (1971) and Fair (1978; 1982; 1988), among many others, focus upon (3); McCallum (1978), Hibbs (1987), Alesina (1987; 1988), Alesina and Roubini (1992) document (4); Kramer (1971) and Erikson (1989; 1990) show (5);[2] and Alesina (1988), Alesina and Sachs (1988), Chappell and Keech (1988) and Beck (1992) highlight (6) and, to some extent, (7).

The purpose of this chapter is to illustrate the first general model which can account for *all* of the above observations within a coherent and unified theoretical construct. In addition, this model leads to the formulation of more stringent empirical implications which are then tested. The empirical analysis sheds further light on the US political economy, a 'light' which goes beyond the insights of the previous literature which focused on a fraction of issues at a time.

Table 3.3 Rate of GNP growth in real terms

	Year			
	First	Second	Third	Fourth
Democratic administrations				
Truman	0.0	8.5	10.3	3.9
Kennedy/Johnson	2.6	5.3	4.1	5.3
Johnson	5.8	5.8	2.9	4.1
Carter	4.7	5.3	2.5	−0.2*
Average	3.3	6.2	5.0	3.3
Average, first/second halves	4.8		4.1	
Republican administrations				
Eisenhower I	4.0	−1.3	5.6	2.1
Eisenhower II	1.7	−0.8	5.8	2.2
Nixon	2.4	−0.3	2.8	5.0
Nixon/Ford	5.2	−0.5	−1.3*	4.9
Reagan I	1.9	−2.5	3.6	6.8
Reagan II	3.4	2.7	3.4	4.5
Bush	2.5	0.9	−0.7	
Average	3.0	−0.3	2.7	4.3
Average, first/second halves	1.4		3.5	

Source: Economic Report of the President (1992)
* Oil shocks

This general model of the American political economy is provided by Alesina and Rosenthal (1995). This chapter is an illustration of the basic results of that book.

The issues

The observations listed above raise many questions. First, why does divided government occur? Is this outcome simply an unsystematic, casual occurrence of two elections 'fought' on different grounds with different results? Or are the voters attempting to achieve a 'balance' between the two parties? Second, why is the mid-term cycle so systematic? Third, how can we reconcile the effects of economic conditions on presidential elections (point (3)) with the lack of a surge in growth in election years?

Table 3.4 Inflation and US administrations

	Average inflation (CPI)*
Truman (D)	3.04
Eisenhower (R) I	1.25
Eisenhower (R) II	1.54
Kennedy/Johnson (D)	1.35
Johnson (D)	3.86
Nixon (R)	4.90†
Nixon/Ford (R)	8.10
Carter (D)	10.70
Reagan (R) I	4.31
Reagan (R) II	3.62
Bush (R)	4.22
Democratic presidents before 1971	2.75
Republican presidents before 1971	1.13
Democratic presidents after 1971	10.70
Republican presidents after 1971	5.03

* Average inflation is defined as the average yearly rate of change of the CPI. Each administration is defined with one period lag; that is, for instance, the first Reagan administration is 'held responsible' for inflation in the four years 1982, 1983, 1984 and 1985. This is done to avoid past high or low inflation inherited by a previous administration influencing each administration's average.
† End of Bretton Woods

These last two observations, in particular, are quite puzzling. The famous 'political business cycle' model due to Nordhaus (1975) has two crucial implications: first, that politicians stimulate the economy immediately before an election; and second, that the voters reward this opportunistic behaviour by re-electing the incumbent.

Thus, while the second implication holds empirically, the first does not, since growth is not systematically higher than average in election years.

Furthermore, is it 'rational' for the voters to re-elect the incumbent when the economy is doing well? Should the voters pay much attention to the short-run state of the economy? If so, how much and why?

The observation about different microeconomic outcomes across different administrations points towards a 'partisan' model of macroeconomic policy (Hibbs, 1977; 1987). According to this view, and contrary to Nordhaus's political business cycle model, the two parties follow systematically different macroeconomic policies. The Republican Party is relatively more concerned with the costs of inflation, and is willing to fight inflation even at the cost of reducing growth and increasing unemployment. The Democratic Party is relatively more concerned with the costs of unemployment, and is willing to run the risk of increasing inflation in order to fight unemployment.

However, Table 3.3 suggests that the difference in rates of growth is short-lived, and confined to first two years of each term (particularly the second). The second halves of the two administrations show rates of growth which are virtually identical. However, differences in inflation rates appear to be permanent, lasting for the entire term.

Furthermore, Table 3.3 rejects another implication of the traditional non-partisan 'political business cycle'. In fact, contrary to the evidence of this table, this theory implies that every administration, regardless of its ideological connotation, should begin with a recession.

The different effects of economic conditions on presidential and congressional elections are also puzzling. Why should the economy influence the two types of elections differently? A particularly striking example of this point emerges by comparing Table 3.3 and Figure 3.1. Table 3.3 reveals that the rate of GNP growth has been well above average in the second year of Democratic administrations. Despite this 'success' on the economic front (remember, however, the increase in inflation!) in mid-term elections the Democratic Party loses ground, as shown in Figure 3.1. Why is high growth good for incumbent parties in presidential election years, but not enough to avoid mid-term losses?

Finally, are all of these observations very specific to US institutions? Or, can we explain the US experience by focusing on underlying variables which can also shed light on other advanced democracies? Is the USA special, or can we apply ideas developed to understand it to illuminate the political economy of other democracies?

The next section focuses on explaining the United States. The one following draws implications for other democracies.

A general model of the US political economy

Alesina and Rosenthal (1995) build a model in the spirit of a 'rational choice' approach to political science and of a 'rational expectation' approach to macroeconomics. The two go naturally together: they both emphasize rationality of behaviour (i.e. maximization of utility under constraints) and in expectation formation (i.e. expectations are optimal forecasts given the available information).

Since the model is also tested empirically, these assumptions are confronted with the empirical evidence. A first, successful test consists of the observation that the model is consistent with *all* the facts described in the previous sections, and provides coherent and internally consistent answers to all the puzzles which we raised. More specifically, econometric tests permit a quantitative evaluation of various effects and correlations between variables. The model also makes it possible to provide the first formal test for rationality of voting behaviour.

A few crucial ideas underlie this model. The first is that the two US parties are polarized. Specifically, they do not follow the same economic policies when in office. The Democratic Party is relatively more concerned with unemployment and redistribution towards the poor and the lower middle class. The Republican Party is relatively more concerned with inflation, and is less interested in redistributive policies. This assumption, which is strongly supported by the empirical evidence,[3] is in contrast with the more traditional view of the two US parties as very similar ideologically and both located in the middle of the political spectrum.

Second, policy outcomes depend upon which party holds the presidency, and upon the composition of Congress. With a Republican president, for instance, the larger the share of the Democratic Party in Congress, the closer the policy outcome is to the ideal policy of the Democratic Party. The analogous argument applies to the case of a Democratic president: a Republican Congress 'pulls' a Democratic president towards the right. Policy moderation does not occur only with divided government (when one party has a majority in Congress and the other party has the White House); the degree of moderation is a 'continuous' variable, which depends on the relative shares of the two parties in the legislature. Divided government is a case of 'strong' moderation.

Third, middle-of-the-road voters use balancing to bring about moderate policies. Since policy reflects a compromise between the president and Congress, voters with preferences in between those of the two parties balance the president of one party by turning to the opponent in congressional elections. Alternatively, if because of the 'incumbency advantage' one party has a solid grip on Congress, the electorate turns to the opponent party in presidential elections. The model does not predict that the US government should *always* be divided: it provides conditions under which one should observe divided or unified government.

Fourth, the mid-term cycle is part of this institutional balancing. Some balancing occurs in presidential election years. However, in these elections one faces uncertainty about the identity of the future president. Under uncertainty, balancing is incomplete. Moderation is completed in mid-term when the uncertainty about the presidency has been removed.

Consider, for instance, a centre-right voter. His preferred outcome is a Republican (R) president with a relatively strong Democratic (D) delegation in Congress. Thus, he would want to vote R for the presidency, and D for Congress, if he were sure that R would win the presidency. However, if there is uncertainty, this voter fears that D may win the presidency. In this case, the last thing that this voter would want to do is to make D strong in Congress when this party holds the White House. Thus, this voter would choose RR in presidential election years, for fear of reinforcing a D legislature with a D president. As a result, moderation is incomplete in presidential years. The same voter, however, can now 'safely' vote D in mid-term, since there is no uncertainty about the presidency.

The sixth assumption concerns the model of the economy. Alesina and Rosenthal (1995) adopt the model originally suggested by Alesina (1987) based on a simple rational expectation macroeconomic model with nominal wage rigidity. This model, which is sometimes referred to as the 'rational partisan model', assumes that nominal wages are set at discrete intervals, as in Fischer (1977). Wage setters form rational expectations about future inflation, which is relevant, since they sign nominal contracts but target a certain real wage. Uncertainty about presidential elections implies that before an election, the wage setters cannot predict future inflation with certainty. They form expectations which rationally take into account the electoral outcome. If the low-inflation Republican Party wins the presidency, inflation will be lower than expected, since the wage setters took into account the possibility of a Democratic victory. The opposite occurs if the Democratic Party wins the presidency. Output growth is an increasing function, and unemployment a decreasing function, of unexpected inflation. Thus, the following testable implications can be derived from the model.

First, at the beginning of a Republican (Democratic) administration, output growth is below (above) its natural level and unemployment is above (below) its natural level.

Second, after expectations, prices and wages adjust; output and unemployment return to their natural level; after this adjustment period, which lasts for no more than a couple of years, the level of economic activity is independent of the party in office.

Third, the rate of inflation remains higher throughout the term of a Democratic administration. In fact, the public knows that the left has a strong incentive to follow expansionary policies to reduce unemployment. In particular, because of rational expectations, after the initial adjustment to the new regime, expected inflation is high enough so that the government does not have an incentive to inflate more.

Finally, the last building block of the model is the idea of 'government competence' modelled as in Rogoff and Sibert (1988) and Persson and Tabellini (1990). More competent administrations are those which manage to achieve higher growth without increasing inflation. Furthermore, competence does not come and go: if an administration is competent today, it is likely to be competent tomorrow.

The voters want to reappoint competent administrations: they choose on the basis of ideology *and* competence. For instance, a left-of-centre voter would typically vote for the Democratic presidential candidate, unless he feels that the current incumbent Democratic administration has lacked competence, or, conversely, the incumbent Republican administration has been particularly competent. Obviously, the more extreme the voter's preference, the larger the differences in competence have to be to convince him to 'cross the line'.

An important assumption is that the electorate cannot observe 'competence' directly: voters can only observe the results of it – economic growth. Thus, when voting in a presidential election, given a certain state of the economy, a rational voter uses all the available information to disentangle the effects of competence from those of 'luck' or misfortune (i.e. favourable or unfavourable exogenous economic shocks). This process of disentangling luck from competence is important because the past competence is a predictor of future competence.

This hypothetical 'rational' voter is contrasted with a 'naive' voter, who simply votes for the incumbent when the economy is doing well, without paying any attention to the different roles played by chance and good management. By imposing certain assumptions about what information is available and on the correlation between growth and competence, one can formally test whether the voters behave 'rationally' or in a naive way.[4]

The model is rather involved. Given the space constraint here, I shall illustrate with an example.[5] Suppose that a Democratic president, who was a narrow favourite according to the polls, is elected. This presidential result is accompanied by relatively favourable results for Republican candidates in congressional elections. In fact, the electorate tilts in favour of the Republican Party in congressional elections in order to moderate the favourite Democratic candidate for the White House. The Democratic administration follows expansionary policies, which lead to an upsurge of growth in the first two years of the term, and to an increase in inflation. In mid-term, the electorate further balances the Democratic administration by turning towards the Republican Party: the voters want to insure themselves against excessive inflation. This voting behaviour implies a non-obvious correlation: strong economic growth in the first half of the Democratic administration is accompanied by a poor show of this party in mid-term.

In the second half of the term, growth returns to its average level, because of adjustment of expectations and in the wage – price system, while inflation remains relatively high. In addition, negative shocks hit the economy in the fourth year, reducing growth to below average. The electorate cannot perfectly distinguish whether the low growth is caused by these adverse shocks or by administrative incompetence. Even if the Democratic administration were relatively competent, the negative shocks would lead the electorate to be sceptical. Therefore, the voters turn to the Republican Party in the following presidential election.

The Republican administration fights inflation and causes a recession. In mid-term, the voters balance the president by reinforcing the Democratic contingent in Congress. In the second half of the term, growth returns to its average level, and inflation remains relatively low. In addition, a combination of luck and (perhaps) competence leads to a particularly high growth in the election year: the Republican administration is reappointed.

Alesina and Rosenthal (1995) note that this story reads as a rather accurate description of the period 1976–84, with the Carter and first Reagan administrations. These authors show that, in fact, this example captures systematic effects and cycles of the US political economy. Specifically their statistical analysis shows that the model can explain in a unified, logically consistent and parsimonious framework all the 'facts' highlighted at the beginning of this chapter. Furthermore, econometric evidence provides quantitative estimates of the various interactions between economic and electoral variables described above (see also Alesina *et al.*, 1993).

These authors also develop a test for rationality of retrospective voting. They test whether, given their assumptions about the dynamic behaviour of the economy and, in particular, of administrative competence, voters rationally use all the available information when voting. Rationality is rejected. That is, they find that voters punish the incumbent when growth is low, without trying to disentangle the effect of competence from the effect of luck. To put it more bluntly, US voters care too much about the rate of economic growth in the election year when voting in presidential elections.

The reason for this negative result for voters' rationality could be that voters may know much less about the economy and its shocks than the model assumes. Thus, what is rejected is not rationality *per se*, but specific assumptions about the distribution of information.

In summary, this parsimonious model, based on the few key ideas discussed above, is largely successful at capturing important empirical irregularities. These results prove that one can go fairly far with a 'rational choice', 'rational expectations' approach to political economy. However, the inconclusive results on retrospective voting highlight the need for additional research effort on this point.

Is the USA different?

Our discussion thus far has focused on the United States. The model by Alesina and Rosenthal (1995) 'takes seriously' important institutional features of the USA: the presidential system, the two-party system, and the structure of elections with a four-year term for the presidency, a two-year term for the House and a staggered six-year term for the Senate, etc. An interesting question is whether this analysis is limited to the United States or can teach us something useful for other advanced democracies. The answer is that it does.

First of all, long periods of divided government are hardly a US monopoly. On the contrary, in parliamentary democracies cases of unified government are rare. Laver and Shepsle (1990) define a government to be unified 'whenever a single party both forms the political executive and commands a majority in the legislature'. In the period 1945–82 less than 15 per cent of the governments of parliamentary democracies satisfied this definition.[6]

More specifically, one can identify two forms of divided government. The most extreme form occurs with minority governments, that is, in cases where the party (or parties) in the executive does not command a majority in the legislature. Minority governments are not a rarity: they account for about a third of all governments in a sample of parliamentary democracies in the last half of this century (Laver and Shepsle, 1990). The less extreme form of divided government occurs in cases of coalition government where the coalition forming the government does command a majority in the legislature.

The case of France is in a sense the most similar to the United States, because the president is directly elected. From 1986 to 1988 and from 1993, the legislative elections have produced a right-of-centre government with a Socialist president.

Other forms of divided government include a division of control of different levels of government. Regional, state, provincial and municipal governments may, and often do, differ in their composition and orientation from national governments.

Parliamentary democracies generally do not have the structure of US elections which generate the mid-term cycle. However, phenomena which resemble the mid-term cycle may occur in these systems as well. For example, local elections held in the middle of the term of the national government may systematically favour the parties in opposition at the national level. Special elections for single seats in the legislature may also systematically go to the opposition. Phenomena of this type are not uncommon in several countries, including Germany, Italy and the United Kingdom. A recent insightful paper by Brady *et al.* (1992) shows that German elections exhibit a form of mid-term cycle.

Partisan cycles in macroeconomic policies are also hardly a US phenomenon. Alesina (1989) and, especially, Alesina and Roubini (1992) present evidence of widespread partisan cycles in OECD democracies remarkably similar to those of the United States. These authors also find a difference between two-party systems and coalition governments. Partisan cycles are more easily detectable and are larger in magnitude in two-party or 'two-block' systems. This is consistent with the theory and may indicate that, in fact, coalition governments may 'balance' partisan cycles.

Can we then conclude that coalition governments in Europe serve the same 'moderating' function as in the United States? The answer is not a simple 'yes' or 'no'.

Several observers have held coalition governments responsible for fiscal deadlocks which have led to the accumulation of large public debts in the last two decades; see, for instance, Roubini and Sachs (1989a; 1989b), and Alesina and Perotti (1995) for a survey. These authors report correlations between the size of coalition governments and the growth of public debt. Since coalition governments are typical of proportional electoral systems, the underlying correlation is between degree of proportionality of electoral systems and public debt.

The theoretical argument is that coalition governments find it difficult to reach agreements on how to implement fiscal adjustments. Thus, fiscal consolidations are postponed until the inter-coalition conflicts are resolved. Alesina and Drazen (1991) and Spolaore (1992) formalize this process of delaying fiscal stabilization as a 'war of attrition' among conflicting groups. The argument is not that coalition governments create budget deficits, but that if deficits appear, these governments have difficulty in choosing a stabilization policy. In fact, the evidence suggests that cross-country differences on public debts became significant after the first oil shock. Coalition governments delayed the fiscal adjustments required by the deterioration of their budgets in the mid-1970s.

To be sure, several commentators (for instance McCubbins, 1991) have argued that, in fact, the US budget deficits in the 1980s are also the result of 'divided government', which created gridlock, rather than moderation.[7] However, the evidence for the United States is much less compelling than that for other OECD democracies. First of all, divided government occurred very often even before the 1980s (see above). Second, the roots of the US deficits in the 1980s are in the 1981 tax cut, and, more generally, in the policies of the 1981–82 period. These two years have had the most 'unified' government of the decade, with an almost complete Republican control of US institutions. On the other hand, it is fair to say that, perhaps, later in the 1980s, bipartisan conflicts on spending priorities might have delayed a correction of the fiscal imbalance.

The point which I wish to emphasize is that one may face a trade-off between 'moderation' and 'gridlock'. At one extreme one finds majoritarian systems, like that of the United Kingdom, with virtually no 'balance': the party which has the majority in the legislature controls the executive and there is relatively little that the opposition can do to influence the legislative process. At the opposite extreme one finds purely proportional parliamentary democracies, where government by coalition is the norm, such as Italy. The presidential system of the United States, with its 'checks and balances' between executive and legislature, may achieve a 'middle ground' between the two extremes symbolized by the United Kingdom and Italy.[8]

The two extremes face opposite problems: lack of balancing and the potential for excessive partisan volatility in one case, and the possibility of gridlock and legislative inaction in the other. The 'middle ground' may reach an efficient compromise by avoiding the problems of the extremes. Thus, the 'lesson' from the United States to Europe is that a certain amount of 'checks and balances' and divided government achieves moderation and avoids excessive policy polarization. The European experience confirms that an excessive use of government by coalition leads to inefficient gridlock, but lack of balancing exacerbates partisan policy-making and policy polarization.

Notes

1 See Lewis-Beck (1988) for a treatment of other countries.
2 See Jacobson (1990) for a dissenting opinion.
3 See, for instance, Poole and Rosenthal (1984a; 1984b; 1991) and, with specific reference to macroeconomic policy, Hibbs (1987).
4 The problem with these tests is, however, that they are *joint* statistical tests of several assumptions on the information structure, on the dynamic structure of the model, on the timing of information revelation *and* of rationality given all the above assumption. Thus, if you *reject* the model of competence/rationality, it is not obvious which of the many assumptions fail.
5 The same example is given in more detail in Alesina and Rosenthal (1995).
6 Data are from Laver and Shepsle (1990) and are based on a sample of OECD democracies.
7 See, however, the criticism by Barro (1991).
8 Italy has recently implemented a reform of the electoral system which has made it less proportional.

References

Alesina, A. (1987). 'Macroeconomic policy in a two-party system as a repeated game'. *Quarterly Journal of Economics*, 102, 651–78.

Alesina, A. (1988). 'Credibility and policy convergence in a two-party system with rational voters'. *American Economic Review*, 78, 796–805.

Alesina, A. (1989). 'Inflation, unemployment and politics in industrial democracies'. *Economic Policy*, 8, 55–98.

Alesina, A. and Drazen, A. (1991). 'Why are stabilizations delayed?' *American Economic Review*, 82, 1170–88.

Alesina, A. and Perotti, R. (1995). 'The political economy of budget deficits'. *IMF Staff Papers*, 42, 1–31.

Alesina, A. and Rosenthal, H. (1989). 'Partisan cycles in congressional elections and the macroeconomy'. *American Political Science Review*, 83, 373–98.

Alesina, A. and Rosenthal, H. (1995). *Partisan Politics, Divided Government and the Economy*. Cambridge: Cambridge University Press.

Alesina, A. and Rosenthal, H. (1996). 'A theory of divided government'. *Econometrica*, forthcoming.

Alesina, A. and Roubini, N. (1992). 'Political cycles in OECD economies'. *Review of Economic Studies*, 59, 663–88.

Alesina, A. and Sachs, J. (1988). 'Political parties and the business cycle in the United States, 1948–84'. *Journal of Money, Credit and Banking*, 20, 63–82.

Alesina, A., Londregan, J. and Rosenthal, H. (1993). 'A model of the political economy of the United States'. *American Political Science Review*, 87, 12–33.

Barro, R. (1991). 'Comments on McCubbins'. In A. Alesina and G. Carliner (eds), *Politics and Economics in the 1980s*. Chicago: University of Chicago Press and National Bureau of Economic Research, pp. 111–22.

Beck, N. (1992). 'Political business cycles, what have we learned?' Unpublished paper, University of California at San Diego.

Brady, D., Lohmann, S. and Rivers, D. (1992). 'Party identification, retrospective voting and moderating elections in a federal system: West Germany 1961–1989'. Unpublished paper, Stanford University.

Chappell, H.W. and Keech, W.R. (1988). 'The unemployment consequences of partisan monetary policy'. *Southern Economic Journal*, 55, 107–22.

Erikson, R. (1988). 'The puzzle of midterm loss'. *Journal of Politics*, 50, 1012–29.

Erikson, R. (1989). 'Economic conditions and the presidential vote'. *American Political Science Review*, 83, 67–76.

Erikson, R. (1990). 'Economic conditions and the congressional vote: a review of the macrolevel evidence'. *American Journal of Political Science*, 34, 373–99.

Fair, R. (1978). 'The effects of economic events on votes for presidents'. *Review of Economics and Statistics*, 60, 159–72.

Fair, R. (1982). 'The effect of economic events on votes for president: 1980 results'. *Review of Economics and Statistics*, 64, 322–25.

Fair, R. (1988). 'The effect of economic events on votes for president: 1984 update'. *Political Behavior*, 10, 168–79.

Fiorina, M. (1988). 'The Reagan years: turning to the right or groping toward the middle'. In B. Cooper, A. Kornberg and W. Mishler (eds), *The Resurgence of Conservatism in Anglo-American Democracies*. Durham, NC: Duke University Press.

Fiorina, M. (1991). 'Coalition governments, divided governments, and electoral theory'. *Governance: An International Journal of Policy and Administration*, 4, 236–49.

Fischer, S. (1977). 'Long term contracts, rational expectations, and the optimal money supply rule'. *Journal of Political Economy*, 85, 191–206.

Hibbs, D. (1977). 'Political parties and macroeconomic policy'. *American Political Science Review*, 71, 1467–87.

Hibbs, D. (1987). *The American Political Economy: Electoral Policy and Macroeconomics in Contemporary America*. Cambridge, MA: Harvard University Press.

Jacobson, G. (1990). 'Does the economy matter in midterm elections?' *American Journal of Political Science*, 34, 400–4.

Kramer, G. (1971). 'Short-term fluctuations in U.S. voting behavior, 1896–1964'. *American Political Science Review*, 65, 131–43.

Laver, M. and Shepsle, K.A. (1990). 'Coalitions and cabinet government'. *American Political Science Review*, 84, 873–90.

Lewis-Beck, M. (1988). *Economics and Elections: The Major Western Democracies*. Ann Arbor: University of Michigan Press.

McCallum, B. (1978). 'The political business cycle: an empirical test'. *Southern Economic Journal*, 44, 504–15.

McCubbins, M.D. (1991). 'Party governance and US budget deficits: divided government and fiscal stalemate'. In A. Alesina and G. Carliner (eds), *Politics and Economics in the 1980s*. Chicago: Chicago University Press and National Bureau of Economic Research, pp. 83–111.

Nordhaus, W. (1975). 'The political business cycle'. *Review of Economic Studies*, 42, 169–90.

Persson, T. and Tabellini, G. (1990). *Macroeconomic Policy, Credibility and Politics*. Chur: Harwood Academic Publishers.

Poole, K.T. and Rosenthal, H. (1984a). 'U.S. presidential elections 1968–1980: a spatial analysis'. *American Journal of Political Science*, 28, 283–312.

Poole, K.T. and Rosenthal, H. (1984b). 'The polarization of American politics'. *Journal of Politics*, 46, 1061–79.

Poole, K.T. and Rosenthal, H. (1991). 'Patterns of congressional voting'. *American Journal of Political Science*, 35, 228–78.

Rogoff, K. and Sibert, A. (1988). 'Elections and macroeconomic policy cycles'. *Review of Economic Studies*, 55, 1–16.

Roubini, N. and Sachs, J. (1989a). 'Political and economic determinants of budget deficits in the industrial democracies'. *European Economic Review*, 33, 903–33.

Roubini, N. and Sachs, J. (1989b). 'Government spending and budget deficits in the industrialized countries'. *Economic Policy*, 8, 99–132.

Spolaore, E. (1992). 'Policy making systems and economic efficiency: coalition governments versus majority governments'. Unpublished paper.

4 *Gordon Tullock*

Rent-seeking in the interior

> In this company, Bill, the people who do well wait until they hear their superiors express their views. Then they add something in support of their views.[1]

At a recent meeting of the Western Economic Association, Milton Friedman gave a paper which, with some very minor changes, was actually a column he had written in *Newsweek* about fifteen years previously. The original theme was that the Federal Reserve Board methods were wrong. Most economists would agree with him that this is mainly true, but there are some who would propose different changes.

At the end of his remarks he rhetorically said he could not understand why Federal Reserve Board members, many of whom he knew were highly intelligent and well trained in economics, persisted in supporting the same perverse policies. This chapter is an attempt to explain why in terms of the internal dynamics of bureaucracy. Unfortunately the same problem will be found in many, indeed most, other bureaucracies. Private corporations suffer from it less than governmental agencies, but it is still important for them. Furthermore, its social cost is great while its benefit for the individual rent-seeker is usually small.

We begin not with straightforward rent-seeking, but with the kind of information accumulated by a person within a large organization, whether that organization is General Electric, the Department of State, the Federal Reserve or the government of Tucson, Arizona. A large organization has both an internal environment and a external environment. Furthermore, its normal reason for existing is its effect on that external environment.

Ford was trying to sell cars to outsiders, and the Federal Reserve Board has a considerable number of 'duties' in connection with the US economy, etc. To carry out these activities efficiently with respect to the outside world, the organization should have good information on that outside world, and use that information to produce workable policies. But that does not mean that the individual bureaucrat needs much information about the outside world.

Consider not the organization as a whole, but an individual member of it. Just for the moment, we will assume that this individual is not at the top of the organization; we will turn to the command group later. Again, we are now only talking about what kind of information the individual should obtain. That is merely a simplification which makes it somewhat easier to deal with the problem. We will turn to the individual's other activities later.

Let us divide the information which the individual could have into two categories. The first of these is information which could improve the organization's dealings with the outside world. This would include general information about the outside world and how it would be likely to respond to various things which the hierarchy could do. It would also include information about potential improvements in the organization itself if these would improve its efficiency in dealing with the outside world.

The second category is information about the interior of the hierarchy, which is of use only to the individual or to some subgroup within the hierarchy. This information would partly consist of knowing who is who and how to find the staff canteen. A great deal of it would be knowledge of various individuals, their respective organizations and personalities and how they would be likely to react to actions or suggestions made by the individual or subgroup. Another important field would be the ideas that are held in the organization, both with respect to efficiency inside the organization and the dealings of the organization with the outside world.

Note that these two categories are not strictly speaking entirely disjoint. The functioning of the organization may require a good deal of the second category of information, and hence this information may in a way spill over into the first category.

Again there will be various specific items which fit in both categories. At a very low level the skilled machine operator benefits himself and the organization by applying his skill. Nevertheless we can in general make a distinction here. Internal manoeuvring which does not benefit the organization as a whole or perhaps injures it is usually readily distinguishable. The knowledge upon which each type of manoeuvring is based is also readily distinguishable.

From the view of society in general or for that matter of the organization the important part of this is the knowledge which improves the organization's efficiency in dealing with the outside world.[2] From the standpoint of an individual in the organization the internal information is likely to be more important. Of course, the individual may make personal gains from improving the functioning of the organization if her or his superiors recognize and reward it. Normally innovators require political skill and a good knowledge of the power structure of the organization to get their ideas applied and credited to them.

Ideally, from the social standpoint, we would like the organization to have an internal rewards structure so designed that the individual will gain most from acquiring the kind of information which will improve the function of the organization rather than that kind of information which will simply help her or him get ahead.

Note that in such an ideal structure, the individual would get ahead faster if he or she did have and use the kind of information which improves the whole structure. Unfortunately, this ideal is rarely even closely approximated. When we turn to the top of the hierarchy we will see the reasons why even at that level there is no overwhelmingly strong motive for providing the ideal incentives to lower-ranking people.

If we look at it from the individual's standpoint, in general the information which will lead to improvements in the whole structure is less important than that which will make it easier for her or him to manoeuvre within it. He or she will get the full 'profit' and feel the full 'loss' of internal manoeuvres, but only a small fraction of the total social gain from improvements in efficiency.

We now turn to a little mathematics. Perhaps I should explain why I find it necessary to use mathematics at all to those readers who do not normally use it because they have no need to do so; and I should also offer an explanation to those more accustomed to using mathematics, because the mathematics is going to be so simple that they might think it a waste of time. Putting it bluntly, the basic reason why I am using mathematical equations here is simply a difficulty in the English language. We are going to discuss things which if put in ordinary sentences would require a great many dependent clauses, and sentences with many dependent clauses are normally unintelligible. The reader with no mathematics can feel confident that he will be able to follow my mathematics easily and the mathematically sophisticated reader need not feel that demeaned by exposing herself or himself to such simple-minded material.

To begin, let a superscript 'e' denote the information obtained about external affairs, and a superscript 'i' information about the interior. We can write an equation to express the benefit to the organization of such information:

$$B_o + fB^e + gB^i \tag{1}$$

B, of course, is the benefit for whatever it is attached to, and the subscript 'o' is the whole organization. Now the benefit to the individual bureaucrat of the same information can be expressed as

$$B_b + f'B^e + g'B^i \tag{2}$$

The difference between these equations is simply that f' is much less than f and g' is much greater than g. Thus external information is more important in (1) and internal in (2). In well-managed organizations information about the exterior may lead to promotion and/or bonuses, but not all organizations are well managed. Even in well-managed organizations, information about the interior is useful to the bureaucrat.

To return to Niskanen's problem at the beginning of this chapter, knowledge that protective tariffs are generally speaking bad for the United States is of substantially no advantage to somebody in Ford. Indeed, in the case of Niskanen it led to his being fired. On the other hand, knowledge that there were several higher officials who thought that tariffs were good for the United States might possibly lead to more rapid promotion. In any event, these two pieces of information clearly have different pay-offs to the individual.

If he or she devotes time to thinking of ways of improving the functioning of the corporation or governmental bureau and is able to sell it to the superiors, the corporation or bureau will do better, but the direct effect on the individual is very slight indeed. This is a very neat example of large externalities and the prisoner's dilemma. As we shall see below, the large organization, if it is sensible, has ways of at least attempting to change the situation by providing rewards to the individual, but there are difficulties. Unfortunately these schemes are far from perfect. Furthermore, they depend heavily on the pressure the outside world exerts on the highest officials, a subject which will be dealt with below.

The information he or she picks up about the interior of the organization, however, has a more direct pay-off. It provides guidance about how to get things done in the organization, who is important for promotion, which superior likes to play golf, etc., and all of these have fairly direct and immediate pay-offs to the individual. They may or may not have some pay-off to the organization as a whole.

Although there might be some positive gains to the organization from this internal knowledge, mainly it is apt to make the organization as a whole operate less efficiently. The information is primarily used for private benefit, both when it benefits the organization and when it might injure it. For example, assume a bureaucrat knows that one of his superiors is very strongly in favour of some particular activity of the organization which actually will be counterproductive. He may benefit himself (certainly at Ford) by making remarks about what a wise thing this is and how wise his superior is in pushing it hard. This would reduce the total efficiency of the organization.

At this stage the two functions seem to be directly contrary to each other, and that fact will not have escaped the people who are at the top of organizations. They, in general, would like to provide adequate incentives to their inferiors so that the inferior will also gain when he or she takes action which benefits the superior. Since the higher you are the more likely you are to be affected by the success or failure of the organization, this improves the general efficiency of the organization. In other words, a set of rewards which makes benefit to the organization correlate closely with benefits to the individual is an important part of the optimal organization.

Unfortunately the superiors may and in fact almost certainly will to some extent interpret benefit to themselves in terms of psychological gain. In other words, they like to be surrounded by people who are pleasant and admire their obvious clear grasp of affairs, and hence normally agree with them. Caldwell of Ford said that was how Ford works, although probably he was exaggerating. Machiavelli said that the Prince should always seek advice before he expressed his own opinion in order to avoid this problem. Unfortunately, people who rise high in these organizations frequently are very good at guessing what their superiors want before they have said it.

Although rewards are an important part of 'optimal' organization, they are very difficult to arrange. They may not be an important part of most real organizations. This is a part of Milton Friedman's problem. Furthermore, particularly in the government, policies which injure the country as a whole may benefit a specific bureau. It has been frequently noted that every time the Federal Reserve makes a really major mistake, its power and prestige are expanded by Congress.[3]

Suppose that you, as an economist from the University of Chicago, are hired by the Federal Reserve Board. You are convinced that the Board's basic policies are wrong and Friedman is right. You push this point of view. There is at least a slight chance that you might convert the rest of the organization. The inertia, however, is immense and the likely effect of pushing it hard is simply that you will find it very difficult to gain promotion and may be quietly eased out.

In terms of your career, going along is the best policy. You might try to specialize in parts of the Federal Reserve Board where the policy does not seem counterproductive. In fact most economists in the Federal Reserve Board are primarily occupied in collecting and arranging data. No matter what your views of good policy, you can hardly be offended by this.[4] This may relieve any internal tension between your knowledge and what you are doing, but it is not the road to rapid promotion. In any event, your information cannot help you and might injure your career.

The difficulty is fairly obvious and shortly we will discuss the types of organization where it is most likely to arise and where it is least likely. For the time being, however, consider the situation. A typical employee who, at least to some extent, is engaging in rent-seeking will agree with his superiors on most issues and try to avoid irritating them. As a result the superiors will rarely hear a point of view which might change their mind.

Of course a person of great personal drive may possibly overcome these handicaps. Napoleon was a mere captain of artillery when he decided there was a weak spot in the British defences of Toulon. He was able to sell it to his superiors and that success, together with his unique willingness to fire grapeshot into a Paris mob, put him on his way to becoming emperor.

Most people lack this type of personal forcefulness. Lee Iacocca seems to have been a standard conformist until he rose to a high rank at Ford Motors. Apparently he then stopped conforming enough and was fired. He then started his career at Chrysler. Since he was president of Chrysler from the beginning he no longer had to follow a careful diplomatic internal policy.

In any event, let us assume that Friedman is correct in believing that the Federal Reserve Board should largely ignore interest rates and pay attention to the money supply. It would then be true that the total costs inflicted on society by its policies are far greater than the gains which an official gets from supporting the present policies. They would be far greater than the gains of all of the officials taken as a group. Indeed, the gain which the superiors receive from not being put to the intellectual difficulty of carefully considering radically different ideas would also be slight compared to the total cost.

It is not necessary to go along with this particular understanding of the Federal Reserve Board's policy to accept the general argument of this chapter. The reader will doubtless be able to think of many cases in which organizations persisted in essentially undesirable policies for long periods of time when could outside observers easily tell that the policy was wrong.

To give one example, Achenson, when US forces were approaching the Yalu in Korea, stated that the Manchurian electricity supplies generated by a big dam on the Yalu were not going to be cut off. This was, as he said, intended to keep the Chinese out of the war. The Chinese, nevertheless, entered.[5] Acheson, however, fought hard to prevent the bombing of the dam even after their entrance, and was able to delay it for almost two years.

The only explanation for all of this that I can think of is simply that the Department of State, having adopted a policy, did not want to change it. Military officers were free to argue that the bombing should occur, but a junior diplomat who argued to that effect would be in trouble.

This gives us a good explanation as to why a lower-ranking member of the organization is not likely to press a policy on her or his superiors which they will not like. Indeed, the lower-level official in an organization will no doubt be psychologically happier if he or she does not consciously behave in a hypocritical manner. Such an official should actually internalize those bits of misinformation which are part of the organization's basic mystique.

Before turning to the higher officials, we should point out that it is not just information that is involved here. Much of the activities of the junior official who wants to get ahead also will be directed primarily at pleasing her or his superiors even if doing so will tend to reduce the efficiency of the total organization. There is, of course, a limitation. If he or she causes a disaster to the organization such an official is likely to be in serious trouble. Grouchy, carrying out the orders of Napoleon exactly after Ligny, destroyed the Napoleonic empire, and, of course, his own position in it. It would have been much better to disobey. As a matter of fact Napoleon would have agreed with this and, no doubt, rewarded Grouchy. But Grouchy was well known to be an unimaginative type.

Let us now turn to the people at the top. The first thing to be pointed out here is that in most US organizations the top of the organization is not really the ultimate beneficiary. Take, for example, a corporation. Economists think that if the corporation follows a profit-maximizing policy and certain other not very restrictive conditions are met, it will also benefit society as well as its own stockholders. It is doubtful that the stockholders care very much about this, however. They are primarily interested in the profits.

The stockholders themselves in general do not play a very active role in the management of the corporation. This is obvious. But the whole literature on the market for corporate control, leverage buy-outs, etc., indicates that market procedures may, if the corporation is run badly enough, lead to the rather indifferent stockholders being replaced by active and vigorous stockholders, with a result that the management is pushed for profits.

In addition, management knows that its stockholders, although they rarely take any active role, can be annoyed by low profits. They are interested in the dividends and it is easy to mobilize them against the existing management if the dividend falls off. Thus the management is, generally speaking, interested in dividends and profits and these translate into sales. The interest, however, is a great deal lower than we might wish. This is particularly true in very large corporations where the man at the top does not really have a very clear idea of what most of his inferiors are doing.

The solution to this has been to offer very sizeable bonuses to high-ranking officials in the hope they will work hard to earn them. Customarily bonuses are still tiny compared to the value of the activities to the stockholders. A $10 or $20 million dollar performance bonus to the head of a corporation like General Motors is trivial compared to the return to the stockholders.[6]

Companies in which the stockholders and higher management are merged are apt to be the most efficient. Unfortunately it is very hard to combine that with talent on the part of the managers over long periods of time. When the man who has built the company dies and passes it on to his children, the odds are very good that his children are much less talented than he was. They have the right incentives but not necessarily the right brains.

Nevertheless, the higher management is to a considerable extent motivated to try and maximize profits, and certainly far more so than the lower officials. There are, as we shall soon see, some severe difficulties here, but let us turn to government organizations. In government organizations the higher management is, in a democracy, composed of elected officials. The voters who elect them are not much more likely to vote them out of office or even change their vote from election to election than the stockholders. More importantly, there is no market for corporate control which can come in and remove them if they are not doing as well for the 'owners' as they could. The only remotely similar function in the real world is the prospect of losing a war. The voters, of course, are very badly informed.

Democracies divide into different types and we may take two extreme cases, the United States and the United Kingdom. In the United States there is really very little in the way of party organization (Clinton is trying to change this. My guess is that he will fail.) Thus, it is safe for the local members of Congress to vote against their party organization and they frequently do. This means that the voters are even less able to discipline their 'employees' because it is much harder to find out what your particular member of Congress did and make guesses as to whether or not this was the best thing for you than it is to tell whether the current government of the United Kingdom is aiding or injuring you.

In the United Kingdom, on the other hand, the parties are essentially corporate organizations who vote within themselves as to who their higher officials will be, but who act as a block in dealing with the outside world. The explanation for this difference is not sociological, it is simply economic.

In the UK the individual MP is very stringently restricted in the amount of money that he or she can raise and spend for the campaign. This is the basic reason for the otherwise silly activity of canvassing which is so important in UK elections. The parties, on the other hand, have essentially no limits on the amount of money that they can raise and hence the bulk of the campaigning is done by the parties and not the individual MPs.[7] The MPs can be quietly dispatched if they violate party discipline. The system shows signs of breaking down, but for the moment UK parties are much stronger than those in the USA.

On the other hand, in the United States we have Republican members of Congress who regularly vote against the majority of the Republicans, and Democrats who regularly vote against the majority of the Democrats. In the United States, of course, they raise their own funds, primarily from various special interest groups.

When we are dealing with politics, keep in mind that we do not really pay democratic politicians very much. Their motives to try to keep their jobs are relatively weak. Directly below the elected officials there is usually a layer of appointed officials who are directly appointed by the elected officials and can be removed by them. In the United States this is fairly thick, some 1,500 people, but in the United Kingdom it is extremely small. Again, these people are not paid very much and quite normally take the job for prestige. The turnover in the United States is very rapid.

The higher-ranking permanent bureaucrats are generally underpaid if we look at the kind of job they have. It does not follow from that, however, that they are underpaid if we consider their personal talents. It is probably true that they are paid about what they are worth, but they are in jobs where we would prefer to have much more talented (and expensive) people.

In any event, it is extremely difficult for the higher officials to exercise any great degree of control over this permanent bureaucracy. Indeed, in a way the permanent bureaucracy has more control over the higher officials than vice versa. A junior official, by leaking strategically selected information or deliberately causing some kind of crisis, can frequently get his political 'superior' fired, whereas the politicians have no power to fire the official. The senior civil servants, on the other hand, have a real ability to penalize junior civil servants.

The Federal Reserve Board carries these tendencies to extremes. The large committee which operates at the top consists of people appointed for long terms, although many of them leave as soon as they have accumulated an appropriate amount of prestige and contacts.[8] Further, some of the committees have different memberships, with the individual banks being represented in a rotating manner. Altogether it is unlikely that this structure at the top is in a position to do very much innovating.

Lower-ranking officials earn salaries that are quite good for an economist.[9] Nevertheless none really has any incentive, other than the public good incentive, to attempt to improve the structure of the Federal Reserve Board's policies. Furthermore, the individual who tries is necessarily pushing against the dead weight of all the others. There is no prospect of getting ahead if he or she starts when young, and every likelihood of becoming thoroughly indoctrinated with the system if he or she waits until older. Under the circumstances 'Do what you have been doing' is the best policy.

To give a very striking example that has nothing to do with Federal

Reserve, there have been two occasions when the price of oil has been sharply driven up over a short period of time by the OPEC cartel. In both cases price control and rationing were adopted. After the first case it was pointed out that the rationing, which depended on historic percentages, had been quite irrational. People no longer went on vacations, with a result that consumption of oil and gas in vacation areas was low and in the places where they were staying home was very high. This meant severe shortages in one part of the USA and a surplus in other areas.

The bureaucrats announced that they had learned their lesson and next time would not do it. But when the second oil price jump occurred and rationing once again was imposed, they did exactly the same thing.

All of this indicates not that one cannot change government but that it is difficult. One should not be surprised if the government continues to make the same mistakes.

Would similar phenomena occur in private corporations? I think the answer is 'yes', but much more weakly. If we look at the history of most capitalist countries we will observe that many large corporations face serious crisis periodically. The companies in the *Fortune* 500 list change reasonably rapidly. General Motors has just had a purge, and the stock market seems dubious of its success.

Corporations face two controls. One is their customers whose influence is somewhat indirect, but who are nevertheless all-powerful. The other is their stockholders who, when all is going well, will pay little attention to the corporation, but may shake up the management if things go badly. Going badly in this case means in essence that they have failed to please the customers, with a result that they are losing money.

In this case those members of the corporation who have direct contact with the outside world are the ones who are most likely to feel that something is wrong. The same is true, of course, in government, but the people who have the direct contact with the outside world are the elected politicians. As a result of the Civil Service Acts they have denied themselves the power to shake up the rest of the government.

It seems possible that one of the reasons for the modern decentralized corporation with a number of profit centres, each of which deals directly with the outside world, is simply to maximize the number of executives who have direct contact with the customers. Consider Ford back in the great days of Henry Ford, in which iron ore was dug in the Ford mines, put on Ford ships, taken to Detroit, smelted in Ford's steel works, and eventually came out as a Model T. Only the people attempting to sell the Model T faced any kind of customer discipline.

The company could, as it did, lose all contact with the customers.[10] General Motors, which replaced Ford as the largest automobile company, had a number of subsidiaries selling different cars and bought many of its components. This put many more of its executives in direct contact with the market, and this may have been an important factor in its rise and the fall of Ford in the 1920s.

The problem here is a special and important form of rent-seeking. The internal manoeuvring within a large organization, unless it is kept under control, is likely to lead the organization gradually to wander away from reality. In lower levels you are better off if you do not 'make waves', and in higher levels a quiet life, together with the fact that you have risen to your higher rank by conforming, may make you also uninterested in new ideas.

The total society must have ways of disciplining these large organizations. Of course, if the society is itself a large organization, as was true in Russia for a while, no such way is possible.[11] The private economy has such methods although they are far from perfect, as General Motors' current difficulties illustrate. The problem is to get such methods into the government side.

So far we have been talking about the behaviour of people in the lower ranks in an organization, and we have rather implicitly argued that the higher members in the organization may actually reward this kind of rent-seeking activity. This is not always true. Consider the higher officials of a large private corporation; once again Ford or General Motors will do.

As the beginning of this chapter, I quoted a man who later became President of Ford on his views of what went on, but the fact remains that Ford did shake itself up fairly thoroughly. I should say that in a recent book[12] I said that every corporation needs a severe shake-up roughly every ten years. This should be a genuinely drastic reorganization, possibly even bankruptcy proceedings, or a takeover. Usually, it is an internal reorganization and is not conspicuous to the outside world, but if that fails the other methods will be forced on it.

As a result, the people at the top will feel that their situation is insecure. They cannot afford simply to go on doing what has been done in the past, living an easy life and seeing to it that their inferiors never do anything which might upset them. A new executive had better not regularly beat the chairman of the board at golf, but he may be able to gain [if he is tactful] by suggesting changes. If the chairman of the board wants to keep his position he should be at least tolerant of this kind of thing.

It is interesting that Ford has a bonus system for higher executives in which the bonus is calculated entirely in terms of the profit of the whole organization and not in terms of the profits of the particular area where a given executive works. But it is still only the exceptionally forceful, tactful and intelligent junior executive who can really make radical changes and be rewarded for them.

I mentioned earlier Captain Bonaparte's suggestion that the attack on Toulon concentrate on what he perceived as a weak point. In order for this to work to his benefit he had first to be able to get it through to the higher officers. Remember he was a mere captain. Even more important, he had to in essence retain ownership of the idea. He could not permit higher officers to take the idea over and then not give him adequate credit. Bonaparte was the rare type of person who could carry all of these things off in the situation in which he found himself, just after the revolution when one would rise fast. Not all junior officials who have radical ideas are able to make the kind of profit out of them that he did.

The private corporation, although it is subject to the same kinds of problem, with junior people having the tendency to accumulate only information which will fit with the existing corporate mystique and carefully refraining from offering programmes which might inconvenience their superiors, has a strong element of discipline. The chairman of the board is almost certain to lose his job if the profit level falls. He is aware of the fact that it is necessary for the corporation to adjust to the desires of the customers if he is not to have that sad fate.

It is unfortunately true that with respect to government agencies this discipline is very much weaker, if it exists at all. In the first place most modern democratic governments have arranged things so that the bulk of the officials cannot be fired and most of their promotions come through seniority, or at the very least through getting along well with people in the immediate environment. The efficiency report is filed by the official's immediate superior and not by an outsider. This immediate superior is quite low-ranking at the beginning of the official's career; by the time the official has progressed sufficiently through the ranks that her or his superior is rather more senior, the official is normally fully indoctrinated into the mystique of the bureau.

There is in democracy something equivalent to the chairman of the board losing his job because there is not enough profit, and that is what we call an election. Officials who disappoint the voters can, and frequently are, removed. The present situation in the US House of Representatives was not characteristic of US government fifty years ago, and we can hope that it will not be characteristic fifty years in the future.

But even if the election process worked better than it does with the current US House of Representatives, it has many defects. The government does not have a simple straightforward success objective like the profit of a private corporation. I spent some nine years in the diplomatic service, and I think that at no point in that service could I have identified exactly what it was that the particular sub-sub-bureau I was operating in was intended to maximize. Certainly there was no way of measuring our performance.

Standard Oil could tell without any great difficulty whether its agency in Korea was contributing to the corporate profits. The Department of State had no simple, easy way of finding out whether the embassy in Korea was in fact forwarding the policies favoured by the Department of State, let alone policies favoured by the elected officials. Indeed, it was not clear that the elected officials had any real policies.

Under these circumstances, even though we do change officials, and they are able to some extent to put pressure on their inferiors, bureaucratic functioning is far worse than it would be in an organization such as Ford.

Turning to the Federal Reserve Board, with which I started, the Board itself is composed of federal appointees with long terms of office. In general, they are not promoted from the ranks of the Federal Reserve itself. They do provide outside pressure and if they can't fire the individual civil servant, they may be able to see to it that his job becomes less pleasant.

This is clearly better than having them promoted through the Federal Reserve hierarchy right up to the top, but not very much better. Further, the members of the Federal Reserve Board cannot be removed even if they make ghastly mistakes. As already mentioned, history indicates that a ghastly mistake by the Federal Reserve Board is usually followed by Congress expanding its power. The reason for this is that Congress normally does not realize that the mistake was literally that.

A number of economists have made a rather specific proposal for the Federal Reserve Board. This is simply that the salaries of Federal Reserve Board members are put on an incentive system. Normally this means that if the value of the money deteriorates their salary goes down.

There is nothing particularly difficult about this, but unfortunately the Federal Reserve Board has many duties other than preventing inflation. From 1929 to 1931 price levels in the United States fell by almost one-third. This was drastic deflation and it is very hard to find anybody who really thinks that we should do it again. We could, of course, arrange that the Federal Reserve Board salaries fell if the value of the money simply changed. In other words, either an inflation or deflation would hurt Board members.

It is not possible to keep the money absolutely stable, and, for that matter, our method of measuring price levels has defects. Thus the arrangement should be such that the failure has to be fairly sizeable before we begin to penalize Board members. If we use this method it would be necessary to raise their base salary above the present level. This change would switch the Federal Reserve Board from an agency which has a large number of functions in connection with banking and the credit market to one that has only one function, but I do not think this would be any great disaster. The other functions could either be hived off to private organizations (for example, the transfer of funds from one bank to another), discontinued totally, or transferred to some other government agency. Most of them are or least should be routine.

The reader will note that this procedure in essence takes the Federal Reserve Board away from control of the elected part of the government. The elected part of the government would have to enact these laws, but once they were enacted it would have little influence over the functioning of the Board. I do not think most people would mind this, but it does have an undemocratic ring. Further, the Federal Reserve Board has control over a very large part of the information publicly available on its own activities. This mainly comes from series of bulletins and tables it publishes. When Milton Friedman and Anna Schwartz began their history of US money they discovered that 98 per cent of all work on the Federal Reserve Board emanated from the Board itself.

Friedman made another interesting discovery at this time, which is a recurrent phenomenon in Federal Reserve Board reports. When the economy is going into depression,[13] the Federal Reserve Board will emphasize its limited influence and how there really is little it can do about the situation. When, on the other hand, things are going well, the economy is expanding and the money stable, the Federal Reserve Board will claim credit for this and allege its policies are the cause of the prosperity. Furthermore, all of these attitudes tend to be reproduced in the press, which has no real source of information on such matters other than the Federal Reserve Board.

We will expect what we in fact see. The Federal Reserve Board continues using outmoded techniques, and does not understand what it is doing.[14] Unfortunately it does not suffer particularly.

Is there anything we can do about this in the government? The direct answer is 'yes', but it is not possible to make it perfect. One of the things that *public choice* people such as myself and Buchanan have discovered is there is no way of getting a perfect government. Since the alternative institutions, the market, for example, also are imperfect, we must choose among a series of alternatives all of which have some defects. The problem is to design things to have as few defects as possible.

The first thing that is to be said about the voting process is that the candidate, almost of necessity, presents a gigantic collection of different policies. Most of these will not be known to a given individual voter. There used to be a member of Congress in Arizona whose views on monetary matters were thoroughly unsound, but who regularly brought large amounts of government expenditure into Arizona. The voters were more interested in the second than in the first.

There is something that can be done about this. We can unpack the jobs so that an individual candidate running for office is held responsible to the voters for only a much smaller bundle of total activities. It used to be the case in the United States that almost all local government officials were directly elected. There might be 80 or 90 names on the ballot in a small town, each of whom was in control of one particular part of the government. This led to the individuals being responsible for only a fairly limited number of activities and hence it was easier to put responsibility on them.

As I said, everything is imperfect. The other problem was, with all of these offices, that most of the voters had no clear idea of who the individual candidates were, let alone whether the man who had been dog-catcher for the last two years had done a good or a bad job as a dog-catcher.[15] Still, it may have worked better than the present bundling system. It should be pointed out that US local governments do indeed have more of this kind of direct election of specific officials in what we would tend to think of as the executive branch, than most national states or in the federal government.

My local county government, for example, has a series of operating divisions as well as a board of supervisors, and the head of each of the operating divisions is a separately elected official. Once more this entails difficulties. We have a department supervised by a 'constable' and I have wondered, ever since arriving in Tucson, exactly what it is that the constable does. Thus my vote would hardly be well informed on him. Still the people who directly deal with the constable, one way or another, are presumably the most important people in deciding whether he is efficient, and he is under considerable pressure to see to it that they approve of his activities.

It is hard to extend this system to the federal government as a whole. For example, the commander of the local air base is appointed through a gigantic bureaucracy which goes up to the top of the federal government. The voters, in voting for their member of Congress and other government officials, presumably take their activities into account to some extent. To regard that as a serious direct discipline by the voters is absurd. Something that can be done is to reorganize the government so that individual voters are called on to supervise fewer officials.

One obvious method is decentralization because there is some genuine competition between governments. Indeed, if what used to be referred to as the common market works out well, it should lead to a great improvement and efficiency of the various national governments.[16] In the United States we have been moving away from local government and putting more and more emphasis on the national government, which probably leads to more and more of the kinds of phenomena I have been discussing. This is one of many arguments for reducing the power of the federal government.

It should be emphasized that the cost of this kind of thing, although hard to measure, should be immense. The gains to the individual people who work this way, say Roger Smith at General Motors, would be trivial compared to the costs they impose. The same is true for the Federal Reserve Board, which undoubtedly imposes a great deal more costs.

In a way it is both tragic and comic that economists have devoted so much energy over the years to designing optimal economic policies to be offered as advice to government officials who are not really very interested. Public choice scholars have been offering advice for constitutions and it must be admitted that we find even less interest in that.

We have a problem, and a very important one. History indicates that governments decay and vanish over time. This is as true of traditional democracies as of hereditary monarchies and dictatorships. It seems likely that the kinds of phenomena we are discussing here are one of the more important reasons for the decay. The problem that I face and which I leave with the reader is: what to do?

Notes

1 This statement was made by the Executive Vice President for Finance of Ford Motors (he later became President) in his final interview with Bill Niskanen before the latter was formally fired. Niskanen, Director of Economics of Ford, refused to endorse quotas on foreign cars, which caused the difficulty.

2 Some organizations are parasitic on or even antagonistic to the rest of the world. In these cases we would like them to work badly, but this chapter is not about them.

3 This is not to say that the Federal Reserve consciously creates depressions or inflations to improve its position. Indeed, a reading of the minutes of Open Market meetings seems to show that it simply does not understand much of what it is doing. There is, however, little pressure on the Board to improve its methods.

4 You might doubt that the data were worth their cost, of course.

5 It is not by any means obvious that the motive of the Chinese attack was to save the electricity supplies, but it is probable that this was at least one argument in their utility function.

6 In the early days higher officials of General Motors were major stockholders. Sloan, the managerial genius, who in a way built the company, had so much stock that daily fluctuations in the value of the stock on the New York Stock Exchange were more important to him than his annual salary.

7 Today the parties' access to TV may be even more important.

8 Manual Johnson has apparently been making a sizeable fortune out of the contacts that he developed in the Federal Reserve. Since I know him personally I am fairly confident this was not the objective he had when he went into the Reserve or for that matter when he finally resigned. Nevertheless, having left, he realized the value of his situation and has exploited it to the full.

9 This raises the additional question of whether academics are themselves very bright. My view is that the advantages of the academic life are such that switching over into risky kinds of activity that most business people indulge in would not be worthwhile. On the other hand, nobody seems to be anxious to hire me for a highly paid corporate job, so perhaps I am just rationalizing my lack of talent.

10 Since Ford owned it this did not lead to as drastic a shake-up in management as might have been expected.

11 War or even the prospect of war, may do it. The Russian system was quite efficient in producing arms except, oddly, aircraft.

12 Tullock, G. (1990). *Economic Hierarchies, Organisation and the Structure of Production*, Boston/Dortrecht/London: Kluwer Academic Publishers.

13 The same would be true of serious inflations, but there were not many at the time they began their study.

14 Anybody reading the proceedings of the Board meetings will have that brought forcefully to her or his attention.

15 In my home town of Rockford, Illinois, the dog-catcher was in fact directly elected.

16 The governments seem to realize this and the common market has expanded more or less equally in two areas, internal free trade and the organization of international cartels in Brussels to avoid the competition which free trade would bring.

5 *James M. Buchanan*

Distributional politics and constitutional design

This century has witnessed a veritable explosion in the size of the governmental or politicized sector of the economies of all states, and between two- and three-fifths of all economic value generated is politically reallocated. Despite the dramatic revolutions in Central and Eastern Europe and the former territories of the Soviet Union in 1989–91, revolutions that reflected the demonstrated failure of socialist organization in the large, there seems to have occurred relatively little spillover effect on the proclivity of governments in Western welfare states to intrude pervasively in the value-creating operation of market economies. The observed movements towards privatization that seemed emergent in the early 1980s do not appear to have exerted lasting effects.

Despite Fukuyama's (1992) challenging claim, the 'end of history', as represented by the triumphant victory of the idea of market organization of economic interaction, has not yet happened. 'Economic science' has not won the day (Buchanan, 1993). Despite what has been the most overwhelming falsification of an organizational hypothesis in history, the idea that market structures create value superior to that produced by politicization has not motivated the behaviour of political agents in Western welfare states. Why not? This simple question must stand as a test for the explanatory potential of social scientists everywhere.

In recent decades, there has been an increasing acceptance of the hypothesis that 'institutions matter' in generating and in shaping the outcomes of all social interactions, whether economic, political, or otherwise. And many subdisciplines or research programmes can be inclusively summarized under the common rubric 'comparative institutional analysis'. But what is there in the institutional structure of modern democratic politics, in particular, that operates to ensure the continuing and successful efforts at politicized domination of economic relationships, in the face of the evidence that much larger economic value can be created by policies that will allow markets to function within generally applied rules but without detailed political interferences?

Why are the French farmers, the UK coal miners, the US automobile workers, successful in imposing costs on their fellow citizens much in excess of the benefits that these groups secure by politicized interferences with free markets? How does modern democratic politics allow particular special interests to replace any possible conception of 'the public interest'? Olson's (1965) 'logic of collective action' is helpful in understanding the results that we observe. A coalition of special interests, each with concentrated benefits, can succeed in majoritarian settings in imposing generalized costs on all members of the polity, costs that may far exceed the sum of benefits enjoyed.

How may we design political constitutions such that the exploitation of the many by the few can be effectively forestalled or prevented? How can democratic politics be made to work for the 'general' rather than the special interest? These are the questions I want to explore in this chapter. I shall do so through the use of abstract analytical models, although the discussion is not itself technical. I apologize for examining features of a political structure that must seem to be far removed from the observable realities, but this seems necessary to isolate and to identify common elements. Even with this proviso, however, I am quite willing to acknowledge that my whole treatment may be clouded by my familiarity with the US republican structure of politics to the neglect of parliamentary systems.

There are basically three distinct ways that political constitutions in democratic polities might be reformed so as to eliminate or at least to reduce substantially the domination of special interests. In this chapter, I shall discuss the first two of these only briefly because they are both more familiar generally than the third and because I have, personally, discussed these other approaches in earlier writings. I shall concentrate attention on the third way of reforming democratic constitutions if the objective is that of reducing the mutuality of exploitation among the many different special interest groupings that describe modern political interplay.

Exit

Why do we not observe the exploitation of all by each that seems characteristic of politics in the everyday working of markets? The most salient feature of market organization is surely the presence of the exit option that each participant in a market relationship faces, to some degree. In the idealized limit, as stylized in formal economic theory, each buyer (seller) confronts another person as seller (buyer) and either party can exit from the interaction at zero cost. By dramatic contrast, in the stylized case of an inclusive democratic polity, each participant confronts all others in every collective interaction, from which no participant can exit. The prospect of exit places direct limits on the amount of exploitation that is possible in a relationship. Exploitation is minimized in market exchanges to the extent that persons may shift among potential sellers and buyers at low cost. In politics, exploitation is much more likely to occur until and unless explicit means are introduced for its limitation.

One avenue for possible reform in political structure is that of introducing at least some of the exit features analogous to those present in markets. The devolution of political authority from central to local units of government, along with freedom of entry into and exit from such local units, introduces elements of competitiveness into politics and necessarily provides incentives for political agents to act in the generalized interests of members, as opposed to exploitative actions against minority coalitions within its membership. Increasing attention has been given to the efficiency-generating features of genuinely federal structures, motivated in part by prospects for effective federalism in Western Europe, but there remains a lack of widespread understanding of the indirect control exercised on the play of special interest coalitions by the very existence of federal organization. Constitutional reform prospects for an effective European federalism seem less propitious at the time of writing than they might have seemed in 1990. And in my own country, the United States, the current policy thrust is presumably towards more rather than less centralization of authority in the central government.

Unanimity

The exploitation of the many by the few, via special interest majoritarian coalitions, can occur only with a decision-making structure that allows political-collective action to be taken without the consent of the exploited or potentially exploited parties. As Wicksell (1896) recognized a century ago, one route for constitutional reform would be the replacement or partial replacement of majority rule in legislative assemblies by a more inclusive rule – at the limit, a rule of unanimity. The larger the majority that is required for reaching decisions, the more difficult it becomes for a coalition of special interests to secure differential benefits at the expense of the whole citizenry. I have written on the Wicksellian scheme in earlier works (Buchanan and Tullock, 1962), and I shall not elaborate on the advantages and disadvantages of this approach to constitutional reform here.

Generality

I want, therefore, to examine the question posed earlier within a setting of a single political unit in which all collective decisions are reached through the operation of a majority rule. In this setting, how can constitutional reform be directed so as to ensure that coalitions of special interests, seeking differential benefits, will not impose net costs on all members of the political community?

Initially assume that there are no constitutional limits on the range and scope for political-collective action. The only constitutional requirement is that majority coalitions are unable to install themselves permanently in power. The constitution effectively ensures periodic elections along with universality of the voting franchise. But once in authority for the designated electoral period, majority coalitions may enact any legislation. I shall concentrate attention on fiscal politics, largely for expositional purposes.

A majority coalition, once formed, may impose taxes differentially on all persons who are not members of the coalition, that is, on members of the opposing minority. And the ruling coalition may then use the revenues collected from the taxes either to finance public goods that yield generalized benefits to all citizens or to finance transfers differentially paid out to members of the majority coalition. In such a setting, it is clear that the dominating majority strategy will be that which involves taxes levied on persons in the minority and money transfers to persons who are members of the majority coalition.

Consider an expectational setting in which each member of a political community considers membership in a minimally winning majority coalition to be equally likely with membership in a losing minority coalition. And all persons are aware of the fact that the winning coalition, once formed, is empowered to implement political-collective action without constraints as to either the type of action or the distribution of costs and benefits.

		B		
		Pays net tax	Pays no tax and receives transfer	
A	Pays net tax	I 3, 3	II 1, 4	
	Pays no tax and receives transfer	III 4, 1	IV (2, 2)	

Figure 5.1 Ordinal pay-off structure for a two-party political 'game'

In this highly abstracted model, with some heroic simplifications, we can analyse the political 'game' as a simple two-person matrix relationship between the individual who is a member of the majority and the individual who is a member of the minority. We assume that there does exist a general-benefit public good that will yield aggregate benefits that exceed aggregate costs. The ordinal pay-off structure is the one that is shown in Figure 5.1. The effective majority, whether this be the As or the Bs, can choose among three separate solutions or outcomes, each one of which specifies the projected pay-offs to each player. The fourth solution, shown in cell IV, is not possible by the logic of the structure. (Strictly speaking, the politics modelled here is not an interactive 'game' at all, since only one of the players determines the solution. Nevertheless the matrix construction is helpfully explanatory for my purposes.)

Assume now that the As make up the winning majority coalition. The solution will be that shown in cell III in the matrix, which indicates the relative pay-offs to individuals who are members of winning and losing sides. Note that in this solution, the As will be exploiting the Bs, who will be made worse off than they would be with no collective action at all. For illustrative purposes, think of the status quo as yielding the bracketed pay-offs in cell IV. The majority will not select the cell I solution or outcome, the one that involves the sharing of the tax costs and the financing provision of a genuinely public good that would yield net benefits to all persons in the polity. The basic incentive structure in majoritarian decision-making is such as to generate the differential exploitation of one group by another, despite the presence of potential benefits for all parties.

The results are, of course, reversed if the Bs make up the winning coalition, in which case the solution is in cell II, with the As being exploited by the Bs.

If the expectations are fully symmetrical, as assumed here, the rotating sequence of results, as between the cell III and cell I solutions, will generate a 'present value' pay-off set like that shown in cell IV. Although this result is logically contradictory in the single period, the expected value of the political 'game' to the players, all players, is zero, that is, equal to the values expected in the status quo, with no political-collective action at all. This result is evident since the rotating majorities take turns exploiting each other, and to the same degree. The simple majoritarian politics modelled here does not take advantage of the opportunity presented by the presence of the public good.

Note that there is no feedback effect on behaviour emergent from the 'continuous dealings' between majorities and minorities over the temporal sequence. The absence of an exit option manifests itself through the continuing dominance of off-diagonal or non-symmetrical outcomes. Contrast this result with that of the market game, in which exit is possible. In this game, the player who is exploited will not enter into further trading arrangements with the exploiter. The non-symmetrical solutions will tend to be eliminated as a sequence of market exchanges extends through time.

Towards constitutional reform

The model of unconstrained majoritarian politics sketched out above is extreme, but the model does, nevertheless, draw attention directly to the structural features that may generate the undesirable results, measured both by failure to achieve the potential co-operative surplus from collective action and by failure of the incentive system to facilitate the survival of non-opportunistic behaviour. Unconstrained majoritarian politics produces the 'churning state', to employ De Jasay's (1985) descriptive term.

The simplified analytical construction is helpful because it points to separate, but related, avenues for constitutional reform within a single polity, either one of which might mitigate, if not totally eliminate, the failures noted. Clearly, the non-symmetrical or off-diagonal solutions must involve the coerced imposition of the action on the minority by the majority. As Wicksell recognized, and as we earlier indicated, any shift in the decision rule towards a constitutional requirement beyond simple majorities will reduce the potential for exploitation, even if the requirement does not extend all the way to unanimity. But the matrix construction also points towards a separate avenue for reform that may well be more practicable. The construction suggests immediately that direct conflicts between sets of participants arise only because there exist potential solutions that incorporate differential or non-symmetrical treatment. The two players must be placed in non-symmetrical roles, defined in terms of actions taken or results achieved.

The prospect of 'winning' by imposing net costs on losers becomes the attractor and it is this prospect that diverts attention away from the potential mutuality of gain promised by symmetrical sharing of surplus. Constitutional reform may eliminate the off-diagonal solutions that embody differential treatment. In the highly simplified construction of Figure 5.1, it is clear that the elimination of differential treatment will produce the Pareto-optimal solution, regardless of the decision rule. If the majority coalition is not allowed to treat the members of its own group differently from members of the minority, it will choose to share taxes and benefits and to achieve the surplus promised by the availability of the public good.

Any move towards reality must allow for the existence of a multiplicity of potential political outcomes, all of which may fall within the set that could be classified to be Pareto-superior to that achieved in the rotating sequence of exploitative outcomes produced by unconstrained majoritarianism. And within this Pareto-superior set, there will be distributional differences as between different members of the body politic. Distributional elements will not be eliminated totally by the constitutional reform that eliminates overt differentials in treatment among persons and groups. But the 'distributional politics' that is constrained by constitutional limits on the off-diagonals is quite different from that which is non-constrained.

Criticisms, applications, extensions and implications

My whole discussion, to this point, may be criticized for the implied presumption that majoritarian politics, as it has historically evolved and as it operates, contains within its rules none of the constraints that the analysis indicates to be necessary. There are both formal and informal constitutional limits upon discriminatory treatment that find their origins in the rule of law, in the precept that all persons are to be subjected to equal treatment under the law. To an extent, these precepts must be appreciated and acknowledged to exist. There are constitutional limits that prevent majorities from going beyond certain overt barriers against discrimination. Any effort on the part of a legislative majority to tax, subsidize, or regulate differentially persons classified by personal characteristics such as gender, race, religion, or geography would be treated as unconstitutional. By dramatic contrast, almost any action by a legislative majority to tax, subsidize, or regulate differentially persons classified by economic characteristics, such as amount and type of wealth or income, occupational status, profession, industry, product category, form of organization and size of group would be left constitutionally unchallenged. (I say this with assurance in relation to the United States, but I think it holds for other countries.) Many possible non-symmetrical solutions are constitutionally permissible and these have become increasingly characteristic of modern democratic politics.

I shall not go into detail with illustrative examples here, but think of restrictive trade policies, pork-barrel spending projects, occupational licensing, and many others. Reform in the directions implied by the analysis of majoritarian democracy here will move towards generality, towards general taxation, towards general accessibility to the benefits of public spending, towards generality in the application of regulations across occupations, industries and product categories.

In summary, my argument here is that politics has lagged behind law in its incorporation of the principle of generality, and that efforts must be made to bring politics into line. The rule of law – this generalized term still carries considerable moral approbation among members of the community. And the central content of this term is that persons should be treated equally before the law to the extent that this is possible, that any discriminatory treatment violates the fundamental principles for a liberal social order. But we have allowed our politics to intrude pervasively into economic life without recognizing that some constraints akin to that summarized under the generality precept of the rule of law should long since have been applied. Until and unless there is some constitutional constraint on the differential treatment of persons and groups, majoritarian politics will surely come to be increasingly distributional.

It is, of course, naive to think that nothing more is needed here than constitutional reform that will eliminate and reduce the discrimination among persons and groups that majoritarian politics embodies. As the historical experience of many countries suggests, constitutions can be reformed without being effectively enforced. Perhaps more important than formal constitutional changes are changes in ethical attitudes that would make attempted reforms workable. There must, first, be a generalized understanding that constitutions are necessary for the functioning of the liberal order, and that the great 'game of politics' is not best conceived as a struggle between winners and losers, is not zero-sum, but a positive-sum game, in which all persons can be net winners. There must be some general understanding that exploitation implemented through politics is just as immoral as exploitation implemented in the private sector.

Finally, I should emphasize that the argument and analysis here do not imply that there is no redistributive political role that qualifies as legitimate. For example, a flat tax, with uniform rates applied to all sources of income along with a set of demogrant (equal per head) transfers, would generate net gains for the poor and net losses for the rich. Such a fiscal scheme would clearly redistribute value. But on both sides of the account, there is a sense in which the precept of generality is applied. There would be no singling out of particular groups either to penalize or to subsidize in a differential fashion.

References

Buchanan, J.M. (1993). 'The triumph of economic science: chimera or reality?' In A. Delfim Netto (ed.), *A Reforma Fiscal no Brasil: Sibsídio do Simposio Internacional sobre Reforma Fiscal*. São Paulo: Fundacão Instututo de Pesquisas Econômicas, pp. 113–24.

Buchanan, J.M. and Tullock, G. (1962). *The Calculus of Consent*. Ann Arbor: University of Michigan Press.

De Jasay, A. (1985). *The State*. Oxford: Blackwell.

Fukuyama, F. (1992). *The End of History and the Last Man*. New York: Basic Books.

Olson, M. (1965). *The Logic of Collective Action*. Cambridge, MA: Harvard University Press.

Wicksell, K. (1896). *Finanztheoretische Untersuchungen*. Jena: Fischer.

6 *Tommaso Padoa-Schioppa*

Government and the market

This chapter is concerned with the relationship between government action and the economy. The analysis will seek to identify some of the general principles that should be embodied in the economic constitution of a European nation at the end of this century. The reference to a narrow geographical and historical field reflects the importance in recent years of constitutional reform in both Eastern and Western Europe.

One of the characteristic features of today's European countries is that they belong to a part of the world which is highly fragmented and undergoing further fragmentation, like Renaissance Italy and classical Greece. This increased fragmentation appears to have revived the threat of economic nationalism and a retreat from free trade.

At the same time, the programme of economic and political union that six Western European nations started in the aftermath of the Second World War has been extended to nine more countries and has made significant progress in the 1980s and early 1990s.

The countries of Europe have experimented with a variety of forms of government intervention in the economy; these have failed completely in Central and Eastern Europe and revealed shortcomings in many Western countries. We are thus faced with the need to revise political and economic constitutions, at both the national and the international level. In such conditions there is a real need to reflect upon the set of rules and institutions regulating public intervention in a market economy. In doing so, I shall organize this chapter under the following themes: the agenda (and non-agenda) of government in the economic field; the two constituencies of voters and markets; the two-tier economic constitutions of European states; and the instruments of government action and constitutional restrictions on their use.

Agenda and non-agenda

The problem of defining the agenda and the non-agenda for government in the economic sphere had been addressed by economic and political thinkers even before Bentham coined these terms in 1780. It continued to receive attention after Keynes (1926) took up the terms again to counter Bentham's argument that government intervention is generally 'useless' and 'pernicious'. Over half a century later, criticism has shifted from market failures to those of government; the pendulum has swung back towards *laissez-faire*.

For an institution like the market to function, two key requirements must be satisfied: that property rights to resources and goods be defined and protected; and that every agent be able to obtain performance of the agreements he stipulates with others. At the outset, the market is thus coupled with the appearance of institutions that protect persons and goods, codify property rights and enforce compliance with contracts. The idea of a 'minimal state' restricted to carrying out these two functions only, is based on the assumption that market forces can allocate all the goods involved in production and exchange efficiently.

This assumption was not confirmed by historical experience. To a late twentieth-century economist there are good reasons for intervening more extensively in the economy.

In the first place there are pure public goods, such as national defence, justice and price stability, which the market does not produce spontaneously and from whose enjoyment it is impossible to exclude those who refuse to contribute to their production.

More generally, the market is unable to bring about the optimal allocation of resources when this requires co-operative behaviour on the part of individuals.

The most common form of market failure is probably that associated with informational imperfections, in the twofold guise of incomplete and asymmetric information. Such imperfections reduce the number of markets and limit the opportunities for profitable exchange.

In some sectors the consumption, production and investment decisions of some agents may appreciably affect the options open to the rest otherwise than through the price system. In this case government intervention can create incentives for the production of goods with positive externalities and discourage those with negative externalities.

Finally, the economy of the real world abounds with instances where competition itself is lacking, where forms of monopoly or oligopoly impose high prices or poor quality. Public action to promote competition can enhance the efficiency produced spontaneously by the market.

It should be noted that, by definition, market failures can only be defined from the standpoint of the common good or, in other words, within the sphere of public action. Individuals do contribute to their determination, but they do so primarily in their capacity as voters.

This is, in a nutshell, the point reached by the theoretical research of this century in support of an agenda for government broader than that advocated by Bentham. However, the experience of the last few decades, in which this broader agenda has been put into practice, has shown that government interventions may have economic costs that are greater than those of the market failure they were designed to overcome. The fact that substantial public intervention in the economy is a relatively recent phenomenon may help to explain the delay with which economists tackled the problem of government failures and the absence, for them, of a taxonomy as firmly established as that for market failures.

Many government failures can be traced back to the difficulties public institutions face in collecting and processing information, the high fixed costs of setting up the administrative machinery, the indirect costs of compliance with government rules and the distortions created by regulatory action, which all too often relies on the presumed omniscience of the state.

Another important type of failure inherent in regulatory action to safeguard competition is what Stigler calls 'the capture of the regulator by the regulated agents'.

Clarification of the role of government in the economic field has been accompanied by analysis of the *instruments* of government action. Instruments can be classified in several ways. At the macroeconomic level, for example, Mundell (1962) and Fleming (1962) have defined the optimal criteria for assigning monetary and fiscal policy instruments to external and internal objectives.

I shall use a classification based on an institutional rather than functional distinction. This may be a more suitable taxonomy for a discussion of the general role of government and the constitutional principles that should preside over it. According to this approach, the four main headings are the *budget*, *public ownership* and *debt*, *money* and *command.* These instruments were developed in different ways and at different times. Their adoption, both singly and in combination, has varied considerably over time. I believe historical experience and theoretical work have put us in a position to rethink the 'rules' for using these instruments, as I shall seek to show in the last part of this chapter.

The two constituencies

We now turn to the issue of the constituency of the government of the economy. The modern theory of government of the economy has its origins in the economic and political thinking of the Enlightenment. Since then politics and the market, in various configurations, have represented the two constituencies to which government of the economy must refer if its actions are to be legitimate and effective. In a democracy government of the economy must pass the test of both. There are many instances of economic policies strongly supported by the electorate being rejected by the market, and of the political constituency rejecting, or accepting for too short a time, others formulated in accordance with the constraints of the market.

The question of good government of the economy can be reduced to the definition of rules and institutions that foster harmony between the two constituencies. Different solutions to this problem have been adopted at various times, with a consequent variety of approaches to public intervention in market economies, ranging from the 'minimal state' to the 'ethical state', actively engaged in providing, if not imposing, what is felt to be good for the people.

The political constituency

In a democracy the political constituency is the 'general will', as expressed in the institutions, rules, customs and associations by means of which individual preferences are transformed into the 'general will'. Notwithstanding Arrow's (1963) theorem on the impossibility of aggregating a social welfare function starting from individual preferences, the notion of the general will is indispensable to an understanding of the history of the Western world.

The two constituencies have different space and time dimensions. By definition, the political constituency coincides with the territory over which the government of the economy has powers of intervention. Its members are those who, by virtue of citizenship or domicile, have the right to vote. Note that for a long time the right to vote was subject to economic requisites – property – which formed a sort of link between the two constituencies.

The spatial connotations of the political constituency are complicated by the existence of different levels of government: local, regional, national and supranational. This means that each individual is an 'elector' of several governments, which may disagree or be in conflict on questions of economic policy.

The two constituencies also differ with regard to the time factor. The preferences of the electorate are formed in continuous time, incorporating fresh information and changes in individual convictions. The same is true of issues and choices that, on either technical or cost grounds, cannot easily be modified in the short run.

A reflection on economic constitution should bear in mind that there is an obvious link between the hierarchy of the actions by which an economy is governed and the intervals at which the political constituency expresses itself.

At one extreme lies the definition of the constitutional framework, which establishes the principles that are to govern the scope and objectives of public intervention in the economy. The procedures whereby the political constituency approves constitutional choices must be sufficiently weighty for the electorate to be conscious of taking decisions that cannot easily be reversed.

At the other extreme, there are the innumerable daily acts of government, on which the electorate is not specifically consulted, which are today none the less subject to a form of continuous consultation by such means as the mass media and opinion polls.

Markets as a constituency

The second constituency reflects the judgement of the market on the government's actions. Some economic agents, such as enterprises, belong to the market constituency but not to the political constituency. Since the behaviour of firms is not directly related to the objectives of consumers, the 'personal union' between the constituencies of citizens and consumers is lost. This is one of the starting points of the modern theory of enterprise.

The ways in which markets have judged the government of the economy have changed over time. The classic example is the fiscal crisis that triggered the French Revolution.

The time it takes before rulers are reined in by the market varies considerably, depending not only on the degree to which free exchange is the main form of economic relationship but also, and more generally, on the level of development of society. The collapse of communism can be seen as an example of the 'market's inexorable response', albeit one that was held in check for seventy years by the constant preoccupation with suppressing or controlling the market's reaction.

The recent integration of financial markets and the spread of information mean that today the market needs much less time than in the past to assess the government of the economy and to pass judgement. It took less than two years for the expansionary economic policy that the French electorate voted for in 1981 to be transformed by market pressure into a policy of austerity.

The market has less clearly defined geographical boundaries than the political constituency and does not have legal signs of membership, such as citizenship or the right to vote. Even where there are no formal obstacles to entry, not all economic agents are present in all markets. Markets can be local, regional, national or international, depending on the nature and quality of goods and transport costs.

What needs to be emphasized is that the close geographical coincidence between the two constituencies that was experienced historically with the nation state (such as France and Spain, which were forged over centuries by the great European monarchies) has been gradually eroded by international economic integration. The electorate nearly always refers to a limited geographical area, whereas the market is increasingly worldwide, thus tending to thwart the autonomy of national policies, in the end even in the extreme case of autarky.

Between politics and the market: the intermediate forms

So far we have identified the political constituency and the market as the poles between which the government of the economy is exercised: politics and the market. The first expresses the citizens' aspiration to be 'masters of their destinies' and the second the possibility of realizing this aspiration and, at the same time, the limits to which it is subject: freedom at one extreme, necessity at the other. The configuration of an economic system depends to no small degree on the specific ways in which public intervention takes account of these two poles.

The polarity of politics and the market is a basic feature of democratic societies with market economies. But these also contain intermediate institutions that operate in the economic field but perform essentially political functions – particularly the promotion of co-operation among economic agents. In contrast to the state, which can use the power of coercion, these co-operative institutions are founded on the consent of their members. Their origins go back to the corporations that featured so large in European economic life from the Middle Ages to the industrial revolution, long before the birth of modern political representation and the establishment of competitive markets as the prevailing form of economic relationship. It is hardly surprising, therefore, that in political thinking these institutions should have accommodated elements of organicism culminating in the authoritarian corporativism of fascism. Traces can even be found in the Utopia of the soviets, in which the 'bourgeois' distinction between delegator and delegatee is eliminated.

Since the Second World War co-operative institutions have successfully functioned in a number of European market economies, such as Western Germany, Austria and Sweden, in what has been called liberal neocorporativism. The nucleus of these structures is formed by employers' and workers' associations and the rules that govern their relations. Exchange of information, co-ordinated bargaining (on both wages and conditions of employment) and joint efforts to predict and govern the effects of their confrontation on the economy as a whole imply forms of self-regulation very different from the *dirigiste* approach to incomes policy and rely, instead, on the government's respecting the parties' contractual independence. Especially in the presence of shocks or extreme uncertainty, regulatory structures of this kind can reduce the costs of the macroeconomic adjustment required. This is an important example of the superiority, in terms of efficiency, of equilibria produced by co-operation in strategy games.

Other forms of corporative institution are professional, trade and employers' associations and trade unions, which bring together individuals or firms with common interests. These bodies often draw up voluntary codes of self-regulation. From the economic point of view they can achieve more efficient equilibria than those attainable by command. There nevertheless remains the need for some general regulation to avoid the risk of collusion exacerbating the market's failures. On the competition front, for instance, it is necessary to distinguish between licit and illicit 'understandings'.

Two-tier economic constitutions and economic federalism

With the exception of the United Kingdom, the countries of Europe have written constitutions. The first such documents reflected the particular configuration of power introduced in North America and Europe by the liberal bourgeois revolutions. They were anti-feudal and anti-absolutist and intended to create conditions conducive to the development of individual activity and to safeguard individual liberty. They accordingly included numerous clauses restricting the powers of government. By contrast, their economic provisions were few and designed to proclaim the inviolability of private property and the freedom of exchange and enterprise. Interestingly, the formulation of many of the fundamental precepts drew on the practice of England, which however did not, and does not, have a single written constitution, but combines rules drawn from common law and precedent with some formal documents of a constitutional nature.

Today, the member states of the EC are notable for having a two-tier economic constitution: one national, the other supranational. Membership of the Community requires each country to comply with the 'Community rule', by which I mean the provisions of the Treaty of Rome and the Community legislation enacted on the basis of the Treaty. Since not only firms but also both the executive and the legislative branches of government have to comply with the Treaty and the ensuing legislation, to all intents and purposes the Community rule forms an integral part of each member state's economic constitution. The entry into force of the Treaty of Maastricht has significantly modified, clarified and strengthened the Community rule based on the Treaty of Rome.

The most important aspect of the Community rule consists in the development of uniform commercial law. A law and a set of principles governing trade and commerce have been established for the EC, with their primacy over national rules no longer questioned. The Treaty grants the Community institutions substantial powers to formulate this law, powers which are probably greater than those attributed to the federal government by the US Constitution. The fundamental objective of this EC legislation is to enact and safeguard the 'four freedoms' embodied in the free movement of goods, persons, services and capital.

The Treaty of Maastricht amends the Treaty of Rome in several fundamental respects. Three of them warrant special mention here in that they significantly strengthen the Treaty's role as an integral component of the economic constitution of the member states. First, by conferring upon the European Central Bank the exclusive right to issue banknotes, the Treaty centralizes monetary policy and transfers the printing press from the member states to the Community. Second, the Treaty introduces binding budgetary rules for the member states. Although numerical targets are established, budgets are not required to be balanced and elements of flexibility are provided. Third, the Treaty expressly calls for 'the adoption of an economic policy which is . . . conducted in accordance with the principle of an open market economy with free competition'. And it further stipulates that the 'activities of the Member States and the Community shall entail compliance with the following guiding principles: stable prices, sound public finances and monetary conditions and a sustainable balance of payments'.

It may be interesting briefly to compare national and EC economic constitutions. While in many countries the constitution concentrates on ends, the Community rule emphasizes instruments, the means of intervention. The approaches of the Community Constitution and the national constitutions are thus complementary.

Many national constitutions of European countries focus primarily on the political domain and accordingly set out numerous economic and social objectives, such as the right to work, the right of workers to participate in the management of enterprises or the right to health, rest and vacations. This reflects a predominant influence of the political constituency.

The Community rule, by contrast, is oriented more towards the market constituency. Above all, the differing concerns of the national and Community constitutions reflect the different positions from which the framers of the constitutions moved. Albeit to a varying degree, all the national constitutions had to ensure not only the proper working of the *economy* but also the full establishment of citizens' rights, which in the modern era include compulsory schooling, decent employment conditions and an adequate system of social protection.

The main aim of the authors of *Community* legislation was to overcome economic nationalism and build a vast integrated market. The Community rule is thus primarily designed to overcome the failures of government of national governments in the economic field. The Treaty does not address the substance of the political tasks of states, such as law enforcement, defence and justice. These matters are only touched on, both because they are dealt with in the national constitutions and because the Treaty itself is not a full political constitution. Thus, precisely owing to its incompleteness, the Treaty amounts to an economic constitution that is primarily oriented towards the market.

Without impinging on the functions of the member states, the Community constitution subordinates the instruments and procedures for the performance of these functions to the four freedoms, or in other words to conformity with a law of the market. For example, the Treaty does not take a position on the question of private property and nationalization and in fact over the years there have been major shifts in policy, such as the nationalizations carried out in France in the early 1980s and the parallel process of privatization in the United Kingdom. However, regardless of who owns them, the Community rule requires enterprises to be run, and the state to act towards them, in conformity with market rules.

One important aspect of the two-tier economic constitution governing the member states is that the creation of a single market and compliance with the rules of the Treaty is a necessary but not a sufficient condition for each state to establish a single market within its boundaries. In other words, the autonomy the member states enjoy under the Treaty does not allow them to gain a relative advantage but does leave them free to put themselves at a relative disadvantage.

The two-tier economic constitution applying to the member states of the Community indicates that, from the economic standpoint, the EC area already constitutes a federation. In some countries the term 'federation' has been associated with the idea of a multiplication of bureaucratic controls and an outright loss of national sovereignty. It is worth recalling, however, that the notion of 'federalism' is based on a principle of 'minimal government', in line with the tradition of Locke and Tocqueville, and hence has next to nothing in common with centralism.

Federalism represents an evolution of the traditional democratic division of powers on a 'horizontal' basis between the legislature, the executive and the judiciary. It adds a 'vertical' division based on recognition of the necessity of different levels of government for villages, regions and nations. Each level of government is legitimated directly by the popular will, from below.

The principle on which federalist minimal government is based goes under the name of subsidiarity: subsidiarity means that government action should be kept at the lowest possible level, 'close to the people' as the Treaty reads. In economic terms this means that the production of every public good must be attributed to the level of government that is responsible for the area in which the good in question is 'public'. The transfer of powers to a higher level should occur only when it is required and justified by the impossibility, due to economies of scale or externalities, of producing a given public good at a lower level.

Of course, while it is sometimes easy to identify the area in which the 'public' effects of a good are generated, in many cases it is not immediately clear how the principle of subsidiarity applies. Is the fight against money laundering the responsibility of local, national or Community authorities? Who is responsible for supplying the public good consisting of price stability? In general, the division of responsibilities between the various levels of government can be effected either by explicitly specifying in the constitution the functions attributed to each level or by laying down procedural rules to decide on a case by case basis. The Treaty of Rome in general adopts the first solution.

In contrast with the United States, the construction of Europe is not based on a single constitutional act but is the result of a process. Even in economic matters for which the Community does possess substantive powers, many decisions are the result of laborious negotiations among the representatives of all the member states. It is none the less clear that the Community represents the kernel of a European federation and not merely an international agreement.

The instruments for the government of the economy

Even a minimal state, one that limits economic intervention to the simple protection of property rights and the freedom of enterprise, must make some use of the four instruments for the government of the economy listed at the beginning of this chapter: the budget, public ownership and debt, printing money and command. Even if the printing of money were taken out of the public domain, following Hayek's proposal to set up currency competition, legislation would still be necessary to organize and regulate the new monetary regime.

Use of all four instruments is all the more necessary if it is recognized that various types of market failure require a wider action by governments in the economic field. However, the experience of economic policy since 'the end of *laissez-faire*' indicates that the economic constitution must not only establish the legitimacy of the four instruments, but also discipline, and in various ways limit, their use.

An economic constitution must therefore provide for procedures and constraints to protect against misuses and abuses of the instruments and perhaps indicate the ultimate objectives of the government of the economy. The development of this theme requires an examination of each of the instruments, their functioning and scope, and their effects on markets.

Budget, debt and public ownership

The concept of the budget as an 'instrument' in itself goes back to Keynes, who highlighted the potential macroeconomic role of total revenue and expenditure and the balance between them. Without this insight the budget would be viewed only from the microeconomic standpoint, as a 'document' listing all the receipts and outlays of the state for the purpose of good housekeeping, that is, avoiding imbalances, while only individual items of revenue and expenditure would be considered as 'instruments'. The budget can therefore be considered as a composite instrument. I shall examine its macroeconomic use as a stabilizer and its microeconomic use in allocation and redistribution.

The budget is a composite instrument also in the sense that the items of which it is composed can be generated either by 'command' (for example in the form of taxation, but also of transfer payments) or by market operations (purchases of goods and services, wages and salaries, sales of securities, etc.).

The economic law to which a national budget is subject is not fundamentally different from that governing a private budget. An imbalance between receipts and outlays has to be covered by debt; if the deficit generates greater future income for the economy as a whole, then it is 'productive' and will be corrected automatically; debt service is charged to the state's current income in the same way as for a firm or a household.

One might then ask why the market and ordinary legislation, including bankruptcy law, are normally enough to impose discipline on private budgets and not on national budgets. The ultimate reason, I think, is to be found in the relationship between the government and the political constituency. This relationship, on the one hand, legitimizes the power of command for the purpose of raising revenue: on the other hand, it solicits expenditure that does not generate additional income. Thus, even if the financial system and the decisions of investors are entirely free and the financing of the deficit is entirely subject to the law of the market, not only is this not enough to impose discipline, but the market may even be misled by the belief that the political constituency will use its power of command to correct the financial disorder it has itself encouraged.

Hence the need for the political constituency itself to establish budgetary rules in the constitution. In other words, the discipline imposed by the market may be too little and too late to prevent mistakes by the political constituency. The political constituency itself may find it desirable to tie its hands through a constitutional rule. Such rules are contained in the constitutions of several European countries and in the Treaty of Maastricht, which lays down quantitative limits on the budget deficits and public debt of the member states.

We now turn from the profit and loss account (the budget) to the balance sheet of the public sector. Here, the public debt is matched by public assets, including the goods and enterprises owned by the public sector.

Consider first the public debt. Just as for a private firm, the market requires receipts and outlays to be in balance in the long run. Purchases of government securities are made by investors on the basis of a free assessment of their return, in which the perception of the borrower's creditworthiness is a major factor.

In the 1980s, when the real rate of interest was universally higher than the rate of growth, budgets were subject to a solvency constraint, and receipts had to exceed outlays other than interest payments. Apart from *ex post* evidence of the real interest rate exceeding the growth rate, many other causes can undermine the confidence of the market in the sustainability of the public debt: the general conditions in the country, the quality of its services and administration, its political and institutional stability and public order.

For investors who are also citizens of the issuing country, an important element of confidence is the knowledge that they themselves as taxpayers hold the key to the resources needed to avoid the bankruptcy of the state, a factor that is lacking for foreign investors. But for an open economy financing large budget deficits in the global, world-wide market, the economic constituency assessing the creditworthiness of the issuer may be very different from the political constituency that led the government to run a deficit. The political constituency itself is under the scrutiny of the wider economic constituency. From this standpoint, a large share of the public debt held by foreigners results in the dissociation of the political and economic constituencies and, other things being equal, increases the control by markets but also the risk of a crisis of confidence.

A rising public debt may generate fears of unilateral, coercive government measures, such as lengthening the maturity, reducing the interest paid or cancelling part of the principal. Such fears may trigger a crisis of confidence. It might thus be advisable explicitly to forbid such coercive measures in the economic constitution. Such a ban would be in line with the Maastricht Treaty prescription, mentioned earlier, to operate with market-oriented instruments. The ban might dissuade a government from taking steps that would soon be severely condemned by the political and economic constituencies alike.

Turning now to public ownership, we should first note that for many public goods, the need for their production to be in public hands is universally recognized: the administration of justice, for instance, and public order. Public property is considered a guarantee of equity and efficiency also in the provision of many social services, such as schooling and health care.

The techniques involved in many public utilities justified the presence of the state. Today that justification is being eroded by technological innovation, which has greatly reduced the scale of indivisible productive processes. Telecommunications are a striking example of this process.

The wave of privatizations in the last ten years was prompted not only by the need to reduce public debt, but also by a change in views concerning the contestability of many natural monopolies and thus the scope for competition in many public services. The transfer to the private sector of the ownership of enterprises producing public goods has nevertheless required the creation of regulatory systems to guarantee the satisfaction of those public ends that a private sector owner-manager would not otherwise have pursued.

The need for a substantial reduction of public ownership has been most sharply felt for the activities open to competition. Three basic reasons have been put forward in support of such action: the diminished importance of the historical reasons for the public presence; the need to raise funds for investment in the enterprises where public ownership is still considered desirable; and, above all, the failure of the model of control based on public ownership, owing to the progressive blurring of the distinction between control and oversight and the increasing identification of the public interest with that of political parties.

Privatization by itself does not guarantee an increase in efficiency. It has to be accompanied by measures that will remove the constraint that may have hindered efficiency under the regime of public ownership.

The Treaty of Rome, by explicitly providing in Article 90 for public enterprises to be subject to the 'Rules on Competition', has made it virtually impossible to run public enterprises in accordance with any criteria other than those of the market. The increasingly resolute application of this part of the Treaty has played no small part in pushing some countries towards privatization.

Money

Contrary to the apparent position of Walrasian economics, money is the *sine qua non* for the birth and functioning of a market. Without money, there would be no exchange and no division of labour. At the same time the sovereign has always considered the coining of money as a function of particular concern, to be followed with care or even undertaken directly. The sovereign was the person who provided the basis for trust in the quality of the metal alloy and the proper weight of coins, as well as the person who from time to time abused the privilege of coinage.

In modern times both the relationship between money and power and the application to money of the analysis based on the two constituencies have revealed new implications and raised new problems. Democracy has apparently put an end to the abuse of the monetary power of the sovereign at the expense of the people by making the people sovereign. The political constituency and the economic constituency have come almost to coincide. At the same time, however, the replacement of commodity money with a token money having no intrinsic value has enormously increased the importance of the fiduciary factor together with that of the state.

Central banks now play the role of the Prince with regard to money and the history of their position in the institutional order is marked by the steps of the debate about the monetary constitution. Ever since the shift to token money, there has been almost uninterrupted concern that too much money rather than too little should be created. The transfer of the central bank first from the public to private domain, followed by its return to the public domain and finally its collocation in a position of independence, reflect the search for an arrangement that would put the printing press out of the reach of those interested in using it to obtain cost-free financing. As long as the balanced budget rule was in force, the bank of issue was safer in the public domain, but the advent of deficit spending undermined this security and led to the search for a form of public independence, embodied in law or even in the constitution.

The debate on money, monetary policy and the *modus operandi* of the central bank has been accompanied in some periods by reflection on the specific question of the institutional role of the central bank: the writings of Walter Bagehot, the proceedings of Congress in preparation for the Federal Reserve Act, and the analyses of Milton Friedman or Friedrich von Hayek.

The evolution of the arrangements governing the central bank has recently been influenced by the monetary constitution of Germany, the country that has been most successful in achieving price stability in the second half of this century.

The German model consists of a set of elements that, with the exception of the Treaty of Maastricht, are still not found all together in any other legal system for the governance of money. In the first place, the German provisions are embodied in the Constitution and not only in statute law. In the second place, the explicit assignment of priority to price stability over other objectives, such as employment or external equilibrium, is in contrast with the Keynesian approach, which envisages the possibility of mediating between them. In the third place, the German model exemplifies a radical concept of independence that not only provides for complete control of the instruments for achieving the priority objective but also excludes lending of last resort, banking supervision, and forbids indexation clauses.

The German monetary constitution has been taken as the model for the states of the European Union. Some of the legislative measures adopted or under discussion in various European countries have been drafted to conform with this framework: an example is provided by amendments to the provisions governing the Bank of France, the country with the strongest historical and legal tradition of a monolithic concept of the power of the state.

Command

At first sight command is the pre-eminent instrument reserved to government and the true expression of politics in the government of the economy since only the state has the power to impose its will and that power stems from the relationship between government and the political constituency.

In the economic domain the birth of the modern state freed economic activity from the 'command' regime to which it had been subject in the corporative regime that preceded it. There was even a separation in society between an aristocratic land-owning class devoted to government and a bourgeois merchant class devoted to the economy. As late as 1926, when Keynes wrote *The End of Laissez-Faire*, the agenda of government was still short.

It was the entry of the bourgeoisie into the state and growing awareness of the failures of the market, followed by the rise of the working class and the extension of suffrage, that gave way to the tendency for government to increase its intervention and use of command in the running of the economy.

Command is not the exclusive prerogative of the state today; it is also exercised by other bodies, such as trade associations and unions. It is true, of course, that only the state is backed by the force of law, and that it is much easier to withdraw from membership of associations, unions and enterprises than from citizenship. But for the economist these are differences of degree more than of substance.

One defence against the excesses of command is disobedience, in such forms as the black market and the underground economy. The two constituencies take divergent paths; the market is again faced with the 'successes' and 'failures' of the early stages of its development.

It is not the instrument of command as such, but the bad use made of it, that damages the economy and creates a fracture between the political and economic constituencies. In the same way as for the instruments examined earlier, the economist's contribution to the work of the constitutionalist should consist in the formulation of principles and restrictions that are both general and practicable and which, when written into the constitution, would limit, if not completely prevent, the bad use of command. Modern economic thinking has prepared the material from which principles ensuring the correct exercise of command in a mixed economy can be drawn, but we lack studies aimed at deriving the general rules for the constitutionalist to apply in regulating the use of command, comparable to those we have for the budgetary and monetary instruments or to the work of Hayek and Nozick, who theorize the complete non-intervention of the state on the basis of extreme postulates.

The first and perhaps the most important rule is that the use of command should encourage or strengthen, not paralyse or suppress, the free formation of prices, which is the intelligence of a market economy. Certainly, all the economic thinking to which I have referred would exclude the translation of this rule into a constitutional provision forbidding any intervention by the government on prices. It is sufficient to consider the need to fix the prices of certain public services. But such interventions have to be regulated with an indication of the cases in which they are admitted and the criteria with which they must comply.

It follows from this general principle that, as regards the instruments to be used, incentives are preferable to command since they do not annul economic operators' freedom of choice or prevent the market from performing its most important function, that of promoting transparency and efficiency in the production of information. In contrast with command, incentives allow operators to incorporate the objectives of the government of the economy into their behaviour. One notable example of the need for such action concerns the protection of the environment.

Freedom of access to the market and, more generally, competition must be actively defended against actions, both on the part of individual enterprises and groups of enterprises and by the state, which through laws or the behaviour of the executive directly or indirectly threaten competition.

Where possible, forms of self-regulation (codes of conduct, the by-laws of trade associations, etc.) are to be preferred to the use of the coercive powers of the state, except for the prevention of collusive behaviour, precisely because they are the result of voluntary decisions.

The need to reduce the area of command does not imply returning to a form of 'minimal state'. On the contrary, this need arises from recognition of the complexity of the objectives set for the government of the economy. It is time to recognize that the idea of being able to dominate the economy through increasing recourse to coercion has proved to be an illusion.

Conclusions

This chapter has dealt with economic constitutions and the general principles that should both enable and limit government actions in the economic sphere. Every economic constitution should endeavour to safeguard the economy against two types of failure: market failure and government failure. During the twentieth century, a vast literature has been produced on market failures, while less attention has been paid to a corresponding analysis of government failures. This is partly due to the fact that our experience of significant and massive government intervention in market economies is more recent.

In democratic systems, the government of the economy derives its legitimacy from, and depends for its success on, two different constituencies, one political and one economic, corresponding to the voters and the markets. The two constituencies obey different logics and have different time and space dimensions. A 'good' government must satisfy both. A 'good' economic constitution is one that embodies a minimal set of rules to establish an efficient equilibrium between the two constituencies in order to avoid, or at least minimize, misuses of government instruments.

Government functions are distributed not only horizontally between the traditional components of the executive, judiciary and legislative branches, but also vertically, between local, national and supranational structures. All these branches and levels interact. For EC countries, the EC Treaty, together with national constitutions, fulfils the role of an economic constitution because all three branches of national governments have to comply with it and with EC legislation based on it. More than for national constitutions of member states, the underlying principles of the EC economic constitution are those of a market economy, both because the fundamental objective of the Treaty is to open up national markets and because the EC level of government is not entrusted with traditional political functions.

Economic federalism is a method of allocating government roles among various levels according to a principle of minimum government. In economic terms the principle of subsidiarity means that the area throughout which a public good is 'public' should be the criterion for assigning government functions to different levels. Economic federalism is a minimal state rather than an expanding bureaucracy.

An economic constitution should not only enable and limit government action by stating objectives and general principles but also define procedures and introduce limits to the use of the four fundamental instruments of economic government: budget, debt and ownership, money, and command. For the first three instruments, historical experience and economic analysis have distilled clear rules that should guide government actions, some of which are now written into a number of national and federal constitutions. As far as command is concerned, economic thought has not yet produced a complete body of propositions that can be used by a constitutional assembly, on how and to what extent government action should be limited.

References

Arrow, K.J. (1963). *Social Choice and Individual Values* (2nd ed.). New York: Wiley.

Fleming, J.M. (1962). 'Domestic financial policies under fixed and floating exchange rates'. *IMF Staff Papers*, 9, 369–79.

Keynes, J.M. (1926). *The End of Laissez-Faire*. London: Hogarth Press.

Mundell, R.A. (1962). 'The appropriate use of monetary and fiscal policy for internal and external stability'. *IMF Staff Papers*, 9, 70–9.

7 *Anton Muscatelli*

International macroeconomic policy co-ordination

The study of the benefits of international economic co-operation has been one of the main areas of growth in the field of macroeconomics in the 1980s. International economists have always been concerned with the spillover effects of macroeconomic policies from one country to another. Mundell's (1968) and Cooper's (1969) two-country analysis, and the contributions to the literature on the monetary approach to the balance of payments and exchange rate determination contained in Frenkel and Johnson (1976; 1978) are cases in point. However, with Hamada's (1974; 1976; 1979; 1985) path-breaking contributions the literature entered a new dimension, as economists began to examine the problems of strategic interaction which emerge once government objectives are explicitly taken into account alongside the structural linkages between economies. This has led to the application of game-theoretic concepts to problems of macroeconomic interactions. Cooper (1985) provides a survey on some of these early contributions to international economic interdependence.

Since the 1980s, the literature on policy-co-ordination has incorporated some of the recent developments in macroeconomic theory. First, the problem of time inconsistency and designing a credible anti-inflationary monetary policy[1] has parallels in the open-economy context. Following the inflationary bouts of the 1970s and early 1980s connected to the oil price hikes, and the cyclical inflationary boom of the late 1980s, most OECD economies now seem committed to maintaining low and steady inflation. An important question is whether international policy co-ordination helps or hinders the achievement of this domestic policy objective.

Second, much more attention is paid in modern macroeconomics to the development of microfoundations in macromodels. In contrast to standard Keynesian aggregative models, representative-agent models allow us to examine the welfare implications of policy prescriptions. In addition, the explicitly intertemporal approach of modern macroeconomics allows us to examine the dynamic consequences of macroeconomic policy in a much less *ad hoc* way than traditional models. The biggest impact here has come in the analysis of fiscal policy[2] given the focus on consumption-smoothing and intertemporal budget constraints.

The importance of these extensions to the game-theoretic models of international co-operation referred to above soon become apparent. First, the introduction of a rational private sector means that the problem of policy co-ordination between governments will also have to take account of the expectations of wage and price setters. The question is then not only whether a co-operative policy can be sustained and is optimal from the point of view of each government, but also whether such a policy improves social welfare in each country. As we shall see, one classic result which arises from the introduction of rational agents is that monetary policy co-ordination between governments which does not address the credibility and inflation-control problem may actually be welfare-reducing. The introduction of time-inconsistency problems can sometimes reverse the usual conjecture that policy co-ordination is always worth pursuing.

Second, the modelling of private sector preferences in macroeconomic models with proper microfoundations can also introduce potential tensions between society's welfare and policy-makers' objectives. Uncertainty in politicians' preferences, random and non-economic influences on the electoral process, and incumbent governments' desire to influence economic outcomes well beyond their period of office in order to pursue their own constituency's objectives, can all drive a wedge between the pursuit of social welfare and the maximization of government objectives. We know from recent economic models of the political process that institutional design can affect elected representatives' behaviour (see, for instance, the surveys in Persson and Tabellini, 1990; 1994; and Alesina and Perotti, 1994). The issue here is how international agreements between governments will impact on policy-makers' incentives and on social welfare. Once again, as was the case for credibility and monetary policy, it is not obvious that macroeconomic policy co-ordination actually improves economic welfare.

In this chapter I shall provide a general overview of some of these recent developments. There is already an extensive literature on this subject, and various surveys which focus on different angles of the policy co-ordination problem. In addition to Hamada's (1985) survey of his own pioneering work and Cooper's (1985) early survey, it is worth highlighting the following contributions: the volume by Canzoneri and Henderson (1991) which emphasizes the interaction between problems of reputation and monetary policy co-ordination; the volume by Gosh and Masson (1994) which focuses on the role of uncertainty in policy co-ordination; and finally, the recent survey by Persson and Tabellini (1995) which stresses how the design of domestic and international institutional arrangements can influence and constrain policy-makers' behaviour. In line with the other chapters in this volume, the aim of this chapter is to provide a survey which is more generally accessible to general readers, rather than specialists. In contrast to some of the earlier surveys it is broader in scope, although, due to limitations of space, much of the analysis is not in-depth and readers will need to refer to the original sources for a more detailed account.

For reasons of tractability, with the exception of macromodelling studies, the analysis of fiscal and monetary policy in the international policy co-ordination literature has usually been kept separate. We have therefore found it convenient to reproduce this division here, with a survey of monetary policy co-ordination issues in the next section, followed by a corresponding analysis of fiscal policy issues. This subdivision does tend to ignore potential problems of strategic interdependence between fiscal and monetary authorities in countries where these two functions have been separated. Furthermore, one would expect any 'real-world' discussion of policy co-ordination issues to touch on both fiscal and monetary issues simultaneously. Therefore, in the fourth section of this chapter we compensate for the partial perspective of the second and third sections by discussing some general, overarching issues which economists have confronted in discussing policy co-ordination. This also includes a discussion of the relationship between the theory of international policy co-ordination and actual observed policy practice.

As we shall see, the actual practice of international policy co-ordination has been mainly limited to attempts to co-ordinate monetary policies. While there are plenty of examples of some countries exhorting other countries to undertake certain fiscal actions, there are no obvious examples of explicit fiscal co-ordination. The limits to fiscal policy imposed by the Maastricht Treaty as preconditions for Monetary Union are an exception here, but their *raison d'être* is more a recognition of the interdependence of fiscal and monetary policies, rather than an attempt to co-ordinate fiscal policies *per se*. It is not surprising that governments have been much more reluctant to constrain their fiscal policy actions through international agreements, as the ability to have an independent fiscal policy is connected with the whole concept of nationhood, and in any case an overall fiscal policy stance subsumes a whole range of microeconomic policy tools and objectives. In analysing fiscal policy, therefore, theory has been running well ahead of policy practice. This does not mean that a theoretical analysis of fiscal policy co-ordination is unwarranted: it is important to understand the possible external effects and inefficiencies which emerge from fiscal interdependence. Indeed, as we shall see below, there is considerable evidence of important spillover effects from fiscal policies in the 1980s. Furthermore, if the trend of delegating monetary policy to more independent central banks in most OECD economies continues, there might be a temptation on the part of incumbent governments to use the fiscal policy tool more actively to pursue their short-term objectives.

Monetary policy

The gains from policy co-ordination

First of all, it is useful to look at the potential gains from policy co-ordination using a simple stylized model of international macroeconomic interdependence.

In a simple two-country aggregative Keynesian macroeconomic model of the Mundell–Fleming type, the nature of monetary policy spillover effects depends critically upon the chosen exchange rate regime. A flexible exchange rate regime will generally produce negative spillover effects, providing that wages and prices are sticky in the short run. Thus a monetary expansion in one country will generate a fall in output and prices in the other country. This 'beggar-thy-neighbour' result emerges from the fact that a domestic monetary expansion will cause a (nominal and real) depreciation of the domestic currency (an appreciation of the foreign currency) and hence domestic output expansion is achieved at the expense of a foreign output contraction.

This negative spillover effect can generate a number of interesting strategic interactions between two countries following some initial common macroeconomic shock. Each policy-maker tries to offset the shock, while at the same time recognizing the interdependence between the two economies. A number of scenarios have been analysed, but the most common one is depicted in Figure 7.1, which shows the options facing each policy-maker following a common external shock which

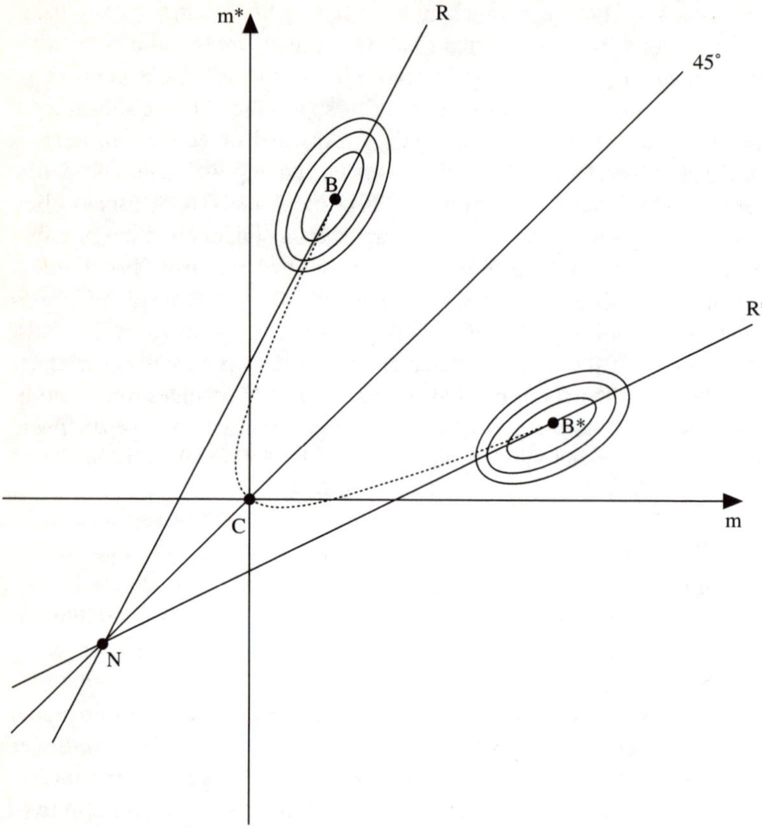

Figure 7.1 Policy co-ordination under flexible exchange rates

raises both countries' price level.[3] The variables m and m^* denote the money supply in countries 1 and 2 respectively, and each policy-maker has an objective function defined over their own economy's output, y, and consumer prices, p^c (all variables are written in log-deviations from equilibrium):

$$
\begin{aligned}
U &= U(y,p^c) \\
U^* &= U^*(y,p^{c*})
\end{aligned}
\tag{1}
$$

where consumer prices are a weighted average of domestic prices and prices of imported goods. The nature of the spillover effects can be summarized as follows:

$$
\begin{aligned}
y &= \alpha m - \beta m^* \\
y^* &= \alpha m - \beta m \\
p^c &= \bar{p} + \gamma(m - m^*) \\
p^{c*} &= \bar{p} - \gamma(m - m^*)
\end{aligned}
\tag{2}
$$

where α,β,γ are positive parameters which depend upon the structural parameters of the Fleming–Mundell model, and $\bar{p}$ is the initial price level shock which has hit the two economies. Furthermore, we know that $\alpha > \beta$, that is the effect of domestic monetary policy on domestic output is greater than that of foreign monetary policy since the latter will occur solely through the exchange rate effects on the trade balance. Domestic and foreign effects on consumer prices are equal and opposite in sign (γ), since a 1 per cent change in the exchange rate between the two currencies will have equal and opposite effects on consumer prices in the two countries if the weight of imports in the consumer price index (CPI) is equal in both economies.

The spillover effects in (2) allow us to express the utility functions in (1) in terms of the two policy instruments, *m* and *m**, and these are the two sets of indifference curves mapped in Figure 7.1. Points B and B* represents each country's bliss point in terms of the two policy instruments.

For simplicity let us assume that each objective function is quadratic in output and the CPI:

$$
\begin{aligned}
U &= -\tfrac{1}{2}(y^2 + \Omega(p^c)^2) \\
U^* &= -\tfrac{1}{2}(y^{*2} + \Omega(p^{c*})^2)
\end{aligned}
\tag{1'}
$$

where the parameter Ω shows the relative weight on consumer prices. The co-ordinates of the points B and B* can be found to be, respectively $((\bar{p}\alpha/\gamma(\alpha + \beta)),(\bar{p}\beta/\gamma(\alpha + \beta)))$ and $((\bar{p}\beta/\gamma(\alpha + \beta)),((\bar{p}\alpha/\gamma(\alpha + \beta)))$. It is apparent from this that each country would prefer to offset the inflationary shock through a combination of monetary expansion in the other country (which appreciates the domestic currency and reduces p^c, but at a lower output cost than contracting the domestic money supply) and a smaller domestic monetary expansion (which offsets the adverse output effects of the domestic expansion). Thus, in an ideal world, each country would like to manipulate the two policy instruments to offset the price increase at least cost to itself.

This is of course impossible, and each policy-maker has to consider the best response open to him, given his own policy instrument, and given the other policy-maker's likely response. It should be intuitively obvious that the only possibility is for each country to reduce its own domestic money supply in order to offset the inflationary shock to consumer prices. Lines R and R* are each country's reaction curve, and show the best response for each country, given the policy stance in the other country.[4] If the two countries do not co-operate, each country will rationally choose the Nash equilibrium of this game which can be found at the point of intersection of the two reaction curves (N). The co-ordinates of point N can be found to be $((\Omega\gamma/\alpha(\beta-\alpha)),(\Omega\gamma/\alpha(\beta-\alpha)))$.

Thus, lack of co-operation leads to an overcontraction in the world economy. This occurs because each country knows that its opponent will try to offset the inflationary shock by contracting the money supply and 'exporting' some of the inflationary shock through an exchange rate appreciation. Thus both will need to compensate for this in setting their own monetary policy and overcontract. The only reason why convergence is achieved at point N is that both countries also care about output, and they recognize that further contraction beyond point N would be costly to both.

How general is this 'overcontraction' result in a flexible exchange rate regime? Unfortunately the result is not very robust, as it depends critically on the nature of the initial shock which the two countries are trying to offset (as well as on the nature of the objective functions and the spillover effects in equations (1) and (2)). For instance, rather than considering a common price level shock, it would be more realistic to assume that an external inflationary disturbance derives from an adverse terms-of-trade shock emanating from the rest of the world. Thus, one could consider the response of two industrialized oil-importing economies to a rise in the price of oil. Such an adverse supply-side shock will, however, have a *stagflationary effect*, lowering output in both countries as well as raising prices. In this case, as demonstrated in Canzoneri and Gray (1985), the two countries *could* produce an overexpansion by acting non-co-operatively.[5] This happens because each policy-maker will want to use monetary policy to accommodate partially the adverse supply-side shock.[6] Allowing asymmetries in the shocks hitting the two economies as well as in the preferences would allow an even richer set of results. Thus, as Canzoneri and Henderson show (1988; 1991), we can explain how lack of co-operation causes overexpansion in some economies and overcontraction in others. This is an appealing result because it explains why, especially after the first oil price shock in 1973–74, some countries which were heavily dependent on oil imports or seemed to attach greater weight to stabilizing output (e.g. the UK, Italy) experienced a major inflationary surge. In contrast, in countries where greater weight was attached to inflation control, a major real exchange rate appreciation took place which ensured that inflation was brought quickly under control (e.g. Germany, Switzerland).

Very different results can also be obtained when one moves away from the Mundell–Fleming-type framework. Recently, Obstfeld and Rogoff (1994) have built an open-economy macromodel which integrates intertemporal maximization by rational consumers in a model with sticky prices. They found that in such a model the major benefits from monetary expansion may not come through 'beggar-thy-neighbour' effects on the trade balance, but through the effects of monetary expansion in raising output in an economy which suffers from monopolistic distortions in the goods market. In such a model, the incentives to operate an expansionary monetary policy would be very different from those in a Mundell–Fleming set-up.

Despite the variety of results, the common element running through most of these models is that policy co-ordination could deliver welfare gains to both parties. The welfare gains from co-operation are similar to those which emerge in most game-theoretic contexts. A Pareto-superior outcome could be obtained if the two policy-makers were to maximize a weighted average of their two objective functions in (1). This would deliver a policy outcome which is on the contract curve (the locus of points of tangency of the two indifference maps in Figure 7.1) and is shown as a dotted line between B and B*. Indeed, if an equal weight is attached to both countries' utility functions in a co-operative outcome, the origin in Figure 7.1 (point C) represents the co-operative solution. Policy co-ordination can therefore remove the bias towards overcontraction (or overexpansion), and generate welfare gains for both economies.

The problem, as with any strategic setting, is whether a co-operative agreement which involves setting monetary targets for each country can be effectively monitored. In practice, comprehensive agreements on monetary targets which would involve mutual accords on monetary targets are rarely observed. However, alternative mechanisms may be found to gain some or all of the benefits of co-operation by focusing on a common intermediate objective such as an exchange rate target.

Turning once again to Figure 7.1, it is apparent that the co-operative solution (C) could also be achieved by fixing the exchange rate between the two countries and by delegating the task of setting the appropriate monetary policy stance to one of the two countries. In this particular example the two countries are totally identical so the choice of the 'centre' country (the one which sets monetary policy) seems immaterial.[7] However, as we shall see below, in practice such a choice may be of considerable importance. Indeed, the issue of whether a fixed exchange rate system should operate symmetrically (with all member countries having some say in the determination of the overall monetary stance) or asymmetrically (where a subset of countries, or typically one country, determines the overall monetary policy stance and the others peg their exchange rate to the centre) is one which has dominated the debate on both Bretton Woods and the European Monetary System (EMS).

In Figure 7.1, however, maintaining a fixed exchange rate, that is, keeping to the 45° line in the diagram, will allow all the benefits of co-operation to accrue if the centre country sets the overall monetary policy stance at $m = 0$. It should be apparent that the centre country has every incentive to do this, as the 45° line becomes the follower country's reaction curve under such a fixed exchange rate agreement.

But can fixed exchange rate systems really be seen as effective ways to ensure monetary policy co-operation? Unfortunately, while fixed exchange rate systems may provide the answer to one set of interdependence problems, they also raise other difficulties.

Do fixed exchange rate regimes deliver welfare gains, and is monetary policy co-ordination desirable?

Fixed exchange rate systems such as Bretton Woods and the Exchange Rate Mechanism (ERM) of the EMS were seen as useful mechanisms for monetary policy co-ordination. Bretton Woods was a response to the unsatisfactory experience of the interwar period, and the ERM was set up in response at what was seen as the unsatisfactory experience of the 1970s in Europe. Under the flexible exchange rate regime of the 1970s, the closely integrated European economies had chosen different monetary policy responses to the two major global macroeconomic shocks of the time (the sustained US inflation from the 1960s onwards and the oil and primary commodity price shock of 1973–74), which led to nominal and real exchange rate instability and to mutual spillover effects of the type described above. However, there are three main problems with the fixed exchange rate regime solution.

The first point to note is that the co-ordination problem described in our earlier flexible exchange rate model is really a problem of targets and instruments. Each country had two targets (output and the CPI) but only one instrument at its disposal. Fixing the exchange rate will remove the problem of interdependence only if each policy-maker does not pursue additional targets. Indeed, Hamada (1976; 1979; 1985) initially specified his strategic policy interdependence problem in a *fixed exchange rate model.* In the Hamada model problems of international policy co-ordination arise under fixed exchange rates because the two countries are assumed to pursue mutually incompatible balance of payments targets.

Second, if a fixed exchange rate system operates asymmetrically, then a shock originating from the centre country can create difficulties for the whole system. The relaxation of fiscal and monetary policy in the USA from the 1960s onwards, and the resulting increase in worldwide inflation, led to tensions within Bretton Woods. Once again we can have a problem of incompatible targets if the centre (Nth) country stops delivering the public good of stable prices in the fixed exchange rate area in order to meet its own domestic policy objectives, and if this is in conflict with the policy objectives of the other $N - 1$ countries.

Partly because of the experience of Bretton Woods, the ERM was designed in such a way as to permit it to operate in a more symmetric fashion. As noted in Giavazzi and Giovannini (1989), the intervention rules of the ERM and the 'divergence' indicator were designed with this objective in mind. However, in practice it seems to be generally accepted that Germany acted as a leader in the setting of monetary policy in the ERM, especially during the 1987–92 period when effectively no realignments occurred. The evidence for asymmetric behaviour in the ERM comes from a number of sources. Giavazzi and Giovannini (1987; 1989) show that Germany and the Netherlands almost never engaged in intramarginal intervention and even their intervention at the margin of the ERM bands was limited. Furthermore, there is evidence that interest volatility was greater in countries with 'weak' currencies. In addition to the evidence from intervention, sterilization behaviour offers interesting insights. Indeed, symmetry in the intervention rules need not imply symmetry in the setting of monetary policy for the system as a whole if the country pursuing a tighter monetary policy (the 'strong currency' country) manages to sterilize the effects of intervention on the monetary base. Mastropasqua *et al.* (1988) provide evidence that sterilization policy in Germany in the ERM was so systematic as to suggest that Germany ran its monetary policy independently of the other countries in the ERM.[8]

Why did the ERM operate asymmetrically? The usual answer is that with the Bundesbank providing the nominal anchor for the system, traditionally high-inflation countries such as France, Italy and Spain (and, in the latter period of the ERM, the UK) could gain some credibility for their anti-inflation policy. The ERM could then have a dual role of delivering monetary policy co-ordination and as a reputation-enhancing device.

Reputation plays an important role in discussions of monetary policy co-ordination, and so far in our account we have ignored this. Following the literature on time inconsistency and credibility in monetary policy design, the formulation of monetary policy should not merely be seen as a game between two countries. In practice, there might also be a conflict between each policy-maker and the private sector in each country. If in each country the policy-maker has an objective for output or employment which is inconsistent with the equilibrium delivered by wage and price setting behaviour then in a closed economy each of the two countries would suffer an inflationary bias. This credibility problem, illustrated *inter alia* in Kydland and Prescott (1977) and Barro and Gordon (1983), derives from the fact that if the policy-maker has an incentive to engage in surprise inflation in order to increase output and employment, the private sector will take this into account when forming inflationary expectations. What happens if two countries with a credibility problem interact strategically in the way described in our flexible exchange rate model in Figure 7.1? The answer is that under the Nash solution each country will experience a lower inflation rate than in the closed-economy context: the overcontractionary bias of the 'beggar-thy-neighbour' model helps to offset partially the inflationary bias which stems from the credibility problem which each policy-maker faces *vis-à-vis* the private sector. In such a setting, where each policy-maker lacks a good reputation for controlling inflation, monetary policy co-ordination can actually be *counterproductive*, as it tends to eliminate the monetary contraction. This point was first illustrated in Rogoff (1985a) and has been verified in more complex models by others (see, for instance, Levine and Currie, 1987).

One way to resolve the above problem is to place monetary policy for the fixed exchange rate system as a whole in the hands of some independent monetary authority, whose objective would be to control inflation as opposed to generating inflationary surprises. A more immediate alternative, if one of the countries in the system has an independent central bank with a good reputation for inflation control, is to make that country the centre country in the fixed exchange rate system. This is effectively what happened in the ERM, with the Bundesbank assuming the leading role in setting monetary policy. A two-country model which formalizes the above discussion by demonstrating the benefits of joining an asymmetric fixed exchange rate system for a country with a poor reputation for inflation control[9] is set out by Canzoneri and Henderson (1988; 1991) and Giavazzi and Giovannini (1989).[10] The pursuit of an exchange rate target as a useful nominal anchor is nothing new, of course, and has been used on countless occasions by high-inflation developing countries as part of a stabilization package (see, *inter alia*, Bruno, 1991; Sachs, 1986; Corden, 1993).

Thus, the ERM can be seen as a mechanism for the achievement of two objectives. First, as a fixed exchange rate system it is supposed to deliver a co-ordinated response to common external shocks. Second, its asymmetry can be seen as a reputation-enhancing device for the high-inflation countries. However, as noted previously, the asymmetry of a fixed exchange rate system can occasionally raise potential policy conflicts where a shock originates from the centre country. The partial break-up of the ERM in 1992 can in part be attributed to such policy conflicts which emerged as a consequence of German monetary unification.[11]

This can be simply illustrated using the model outlined previously. Suppose that the two countries enter a fixed exchange rate system such as that illustrated in Figure 7.2, where the task of setting monetary policy falls to the unstarred country.[12] Thus, under a co-operative solution $m = 0$ is set, and the follower country sets $m^* = 0$ in order to maintain a fixed exchange rate at point (C). Next let us suppose that an asymmetric inflation shock hits the centre country.[13] This will shift the reaction curve R upwards to R′ (together with B to B′ and the whole of the centre country's objective function contours) and will mean that the initial monetary policy setting (C) is no longer optimal for the centre country. Under the rules of the game, the centre can choose to set m so as to maximize its (new) objective function, and as a leader will choose point L^G, which will involve a monetary contraction relative to C, and in order to defend the chosen parity the other country will have to follow. Intuitively, an inflationary shock in Germany which called for a domestic monetary contraction would have to be followed by all the other ERM members. The optimal solution to such an asymmetric shock is of course not L^G, but to choose a new co-operative solution C^R, which is on the new contract curve between the two countries. This lies on a different 45° line and implies an exchange rate

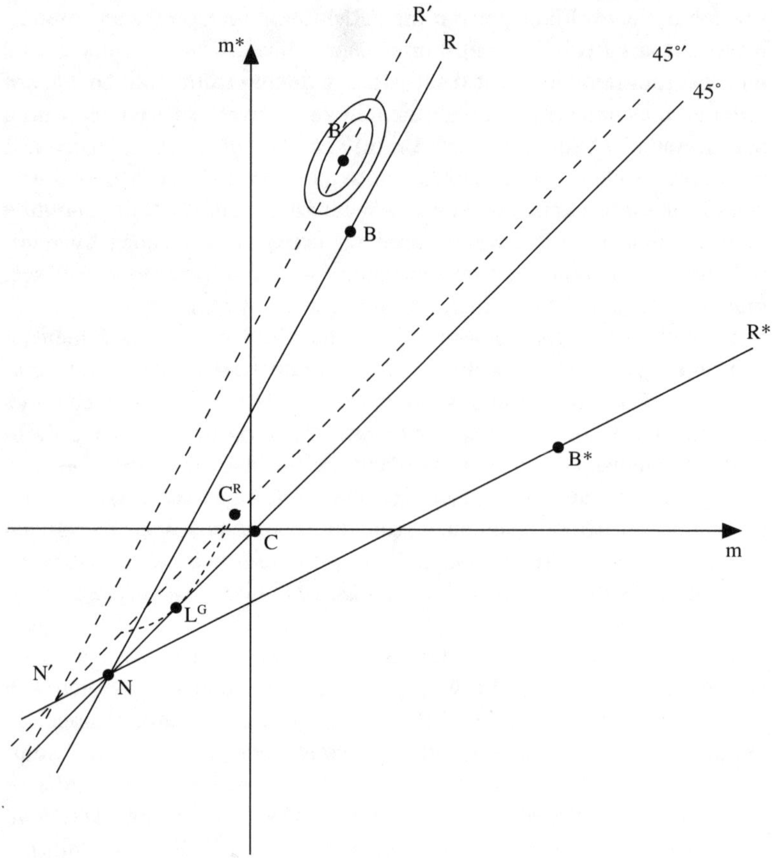

Figure 7.2 Asymmetric shocks, co-operation and parity realignments

realignment. Thus, the optimal co-operative solution to an asymmetric shock is not to maintain a fixed parity.

All this raises the question why the optimal response of a realignment following the inflationary shock of German monetary unification was not chosen. The most plausible explanation is that the follower countries felt that this might have adversely affected their reputational gains. There might also have been a reluctance to undermine the hard-ERM regime by resuming realignments, especially if the hard ERM was seen as a necessary precursor to eventual European Monetary Union (EMU). This is puzzling as most official descriptions of the process towards EMU did not seem to preclude realignments in the run-up to it (see Delors Report, 1989). Furthermore, it can be shown that in the presence of unemployment persistence, a delay in the realignment can actually reduce the credibility of the followers' policy stance (see Drazen and Masson, 1994).

In terms of the above model, the use of the ERM as a reputation-enhancing device came into conflict with the pursuit of each country's domestic objectives and with its role as a proxy for monetary policy co-ordination.[14] It should not be surprising that foreign exchange markets saw such tensions as offering a good one-way speculative bet, thereby bringing about the partial downfall of the ERM in 1992 and 1993.

This takes us on to the third problem with fixed exchange rate systems as proxies for monetary policy co-ordination. Increasing capital mobility has made it much more difficult for countries effectively to defend announced exchange rate parities against speculative attacks. Once again, the Bretton Woods experience was taken into account when designing the ERM. Bilateral interventions, together with the various financing facilities (including unlimited initial credit lines for intervention under the very short-term financing facility) were supposed to make the ERM more resistant to speculative attacks. These arrangements were also strengthened in 1987. But all the tactical weapons in the world cannot provide a way out of a strategic error. A number of economists foresaw these difficulties well in advance of the crises of 1992 and 1993. For instance, Kenen (1988) states:

> But two trends may be working to make realignments more difficult in the future, which could also impair the health of the adjustable peg. First, markets seem to be learning how to predict realignments, and the figures on reserve flows . . . suggest that anticipatory capital flows have been getting larger. Second, the movement to eliminate capital controls . . . These trends could impair the viability of the EMS if they lead the authorities to postpone realignments merely to disappoint the market's expectations . . . it would sometimes make sense to realign exchange rates before it is perfectly clear that a realignment is required by a change in fundamentals, even at the risk of having to reverse it later.

An added difficulty with a high degree of capital mobility is that it tends to enhance the potential conflicts in a fixed exchange rate system. A high degree of capital mobility also implies that sterilization policies become less effective. Thus, if the centre country wishes to continue to pursue its domestic policy objectives as in Figure 7.2, and if a realignment is ruled out by the follower country, continued bilateral intervention in the face of massive capital flows will impair the centre country's pursuit of its chosen policy stance. In this type of situation financial markets may feel that the monetary authorities of the centre country will not be willing to resist such speculative pressures. Similarly, as suggested previously, if follower countries delay realignments and have to raise interest rates to defend their parity when their economies suffer a high degree of unemployment persistence then this may be seen as politically untenable (see Drazen and Masson, 1994; Lockwood *et al.*, 1993). In such circumstances capital markets can generate a self-fulfilling speculative attack. This has strengthened calls for some restrictions on capital movements (see Eichengreen *et al.*, 1995a; 1995b).

So far we have highlighted some of the difficulties in pursuing monetary policy co-ordination, focusing on the possible role of fixed exchange rate systems as proxies for full-blown (symmetric) policy co-ordination and the potential problems involved. We shall return to a broader discussion of monetary policy co-ordination schemes in the section after next. However, before that, we turn our attention to fiscal policy issues.

Fiscal policy

The potential benefits from co-operation

As in the case of monetary policy, economic interdependence arising from fiscal policy spillover effects can yield potential gains from co-operation. The analytical techniques which can be applied here to show the benefits of co-operation are similar to those shown in the previous section and in Figures 7.1 and 7.2, and so we shall not repeat them here. Instead we shall concentrate on identifying the likely sources of the fiscal spillover effects and the potential welfare gains from co-operation.

It should be made clear at the outset that fiscal policy co-ordination raises several issues which we did not have to confront with monetary policy. First, we cannot really speak of a single 'fiscal instrument' since in practice the nature of the interdependence will depend critically on the design of the taxation or expenditure policy being considered. In this chapter we shall confine our attention to a subset of the likely channels of interdependence. Second, as noted in the introduction, there is a lack of consensus over the appropriate model to use to analyse fiscal policy. Fiscal spillover effects will differ considerably depending on whether we focus on a traditional Keynesian aggregative model (such as Fleming–Mundell-type models) or on representative-agent models based on rational forward-looking consumers.

There are also common elements which are worth emphasizing. In particular, we saw that the analysis of monetary policy involved the interaction (and potential conflict) between the institutional arrangements to achieve international policy co-ordination and the domestic institutional arrangements to maintain credibility. Similar problems arise here, and the result is that, once again, there is no presumption that fiscal policy co-ordination will enhance social welfare in both countries. This is the case where domestic political institutions do not exert sufficient discipline on each government and where international linkages in the absence of co-operation usefully limit the scope for government action.

We start by looking at the aggregative models. The spillover effects from fiscal policy on the aggregate demand side will operate under fixed and flexible exchange rates through the trade balance. These could be analysed using the same framework as that outlined in the previous section and Figure 7.1. However, the main interest in fiscal policy spillover effects lies in the fact that they might operate even in the long run, even with flexible wages and prices. One key spillover effect which has received some attention has been the impact of the real exchange rate on the equilibrium rate of unemployment via its effect on the wedge between the product real wage and the consumer real wage (see, for instance, Bruce and Purvis, 1985; Bruno and Sachs, 1985; Bean *et al.*, 1986; Alogoskoufis and Martin, 1991). Higher government spending in such a model can generate lower unemployment by appreciating the real exchange rate, which drives a bigger wedge between producer prices and consumer prices and allows a lower real product wage to coexist with a higher or unchanged real consumer wage. Fiscal expansion which takes the form of lower income taxation or social security payments can also achieve a similar effect by raising real disposable income relative to labour costs.

In so far as these effects are present, they can potentially explain a number of phenomena. Alogoskoufis and Martin (1991) and Alogoskoufis and Varangis (1992) look at the role of these factors in explaining North–South macroeconomic interactions (see also Cristini, 1995; Muscatelli, 1995a). Undoubtedly the sudden deterioration in the terms of trade of the developed economies (the North) relative to the developing economies (the South) following the commodity and oil price shock of the early 1970s created an adverse supply shock, and this is well documented (see Bruno and Sachs, 1985; Layard *et al.*, 1991). However, Alogoskoufis and Martin (1991) also attribute the differential performance of unemployment in Europe and the USA to the greater willingness on the latter's part to use expansionary fiscal policies in the 1980s.[15] This is also a theme in Blanchard (1987) and Cohen and Wyplosz (1990; 1991) who suggest that European fiscal policy might have been too inactive in the 1980s relative to that of the USA.

However, as noted by Sachs (1985), if all individual governments respond to an adverse employment shock by seeking to exploit this fiscal policy link, an overexpansionary equilibrium[16] could occur. In the absence of co-operation both countries would seek to undertake a fiscal expansion. However, under the Nash solution no country is able to reduce unemployment as the real exchange rate between the two remains unchanged. The only net result is an excessive fiscal expansion with consequences for each country's deficit and world inflation. Ermisch and Muscatelli (1993) construct a model along these lines where each government targets unemployment and the CPI in the face of a labour supply disturbance. This simple stylized model shows the potential dangers of an overactive fiscal policy especially where there are constraints on monetary policy (e.g. within a fixed exchange rate system or a monetary union).

The problem is that such global theories of unemployment determination are too ambitious. Labour market differences between countries provide an adequate explanation of unemployment differences. Furthermore, the main problem with all the models built around 'the wedge' is that empirical support for the 'wedge' effect is mixed (see Newell and Symons, 1985; Bean *et al.*, 1986; Layard *et al.*, 1991). It seems unlikely that policy-makers have knowingly been trying to exploit this effect. For instance, we would probably not argue that the dollar appreciation of the Reagan–Volcker years was a deliberately engineered policy mix with an eye to appreciating the real dollar exchange rate!

However, the spillover effects of fiscal policy may be more extensive than those suggested by the simple Keynesian aggregative model sketched out above. Further refinements of the microfoundations of the demand and supply side of open-economy models have led to a richer variety of results[17] (see, for instance, Frenkel and Razin, 1987; Obstfeld and Rogoff, 1994). Here we shall concentrate on one possible channel of transmission which could have been significant in the last two decades, based on the structuralist macroeconomic model developed in Phelps (1995).

Consider a closed economy in which there is an expansion of public debt due to a temporary increase in expenditures or due to a policy of short-term tax cuts. In finite-horizon models of consumption behaviour where the Ricardian equivalence theorem does not hold,[18] such as the Blanchard–Yaari perpetual youth model (see Blanchard, 1985; Blanchard and Fischer, 1989), this will lead to an increase in the interest rate. Rising real interest rates will then impact negatively on labour demand through a variety of channels. One channel might be a reduced rate of physical investment,[19] as real prices of capital assets fall, but one can also think of a reduction in less visible, more subtle types of investment, such as workforce training. Thus, the equilibrium rate of unemployment (the NAIRU) can be expected to rise in those economies (such as in Europe) where there is considerable real wage rigidity. Where real wages are less rigid, the fall in labour demand will be partly accommodated by a fall in real wages.

This mechanism can be readily extended to open-economy models. Where there is a global fiscal expansion and an increase in public debt this will lead to a world-wide increase in the equilibrium rate of unemployment. The merit of such a structural explanation of unemployment is that it complements more traditional models of hysteresis and slow adjustment, by providing an explanation for the intractability of the unemployment problem in Europe in the 1980s.[20] It also leads to interesting strategic interactions. At the level of a single economy, a policy-maker wishing to increase domestic employment through an expansionary fiscal policy[21] may not take into account the overall impact of his policy actions on the world-wide rate of interest, and a co-ordination failure can ensue which leads to a global increase in the NAIRU. A concerted policy action to avoid such fiscal overexpansion could help to eliminate the problem.

Political institutions, fiscal policy, and problems arising from co-operation

Earlier we saw that by not treating the government as a benevolent social planner and by introducing a source of conflict between the policy-maker's objectives and the preferences of the private sector, monetary policy co-ordination might prove to be counterproductive. Essentially the key point is whether policy actions in each country are subject to some distortion due to the domestic institutional setting. If this is the case, the lack of policy co-ordination may actually partially correct the domestic distortion, and policy co-ordination could be undesirable. Similar issues arise in the case of fiscal policy once we consider the political institutional setting within which fiscal policy is set.

Indeed, one defect of the analysis so far in this section is that it has totally ignored the objectives of a politically motivated government. If we want to explain what motivates fiscal policy, we ultimately have to look to political preferences and electoral objectives as key driving forces. Thus, governments may pursue distorted policies because they have partisan objectives (policy objectives which match the preferences of *a* part of society), or because they are office-motivated and are pursuing short-term benefits for electoral purposes. When co-operating over fiscal policies such governments may collude against the interests of the private sector (for an interesting exposition, see Vaubel, 1985).

The issues discussed here were first presented by Tabellini (1990) in an open-economy extension of an earlier literature on how electoral cycles can create a bias towards budget deficits (see, *inter alia*, Persson and Svensson, 1989; Alesina and Tabellini, 1990; Tabellini and Alesina, 1990). The bias towards deficits in each country is a product of a two-party system where each party has different preferences on the optimal allocation of public expenditures on two different public goods. This conflict over the composition of government spending and the uncertainty over the electoral outcome forces each party to act strategically when in power. They will generally run deficits in order to constrain the policy options of future governments when they are in opposition.

The open-economy element operates through the terms of trade. The debt in each country is indexed to a composite consumption good (which contains domestic and foreign goods in fixed proportions). Thus an expansionary fiscal policy in one country causes an appreciation of the real exchange rate, and, through the debt indexation mechanism, raises the cost of issuing debt. Thus, the terms-of-trade effect of running a fiscal deficit means that a country will find it more costly to act unilaterally on fiscal policy.

What are the implications for policy co-ordination? If the two countries co-ordinate their expansion, the terms-of-trade effect disappears and this would then remove this constraint on excessive fiscal deficits. In this sense co-ordination could be counterproductive. However, as Tabellini (1990) notes, this result could be reversed. A fiscal expansion in each country also raises the world interest rate, and co-operation can internalize this negative externality. Thus, co-operation may or may not be beneficial depending on whether the terms-of-trade effect or the interest rate effect dominates.

The model as sketched out by Tabellini (1990) might seem too simple at first sight to explain real-world phenomena. But it should be noted that this model can be generalized without changing its main conclusions. If we allow international borrowing, then the (intertemporal) terms-of-trade effect would constrain a country from running fiscal deficits as a debtor country is penalized by an increase in the world interest rate (see Frenkel and Razin, 1987; Frenkel *et al.*, 1991). On the other hand, a co-ordinated fiscal expansion would partially release the constraint on the two policy-makers.

Policy co-ordination: from theory to practice

Our analysis so far has identified some possible sources of welfare gains and losses from policy co-ordination in the spheres of both monetary and fiscal policy. In outlining a variety of theoretical models we have tended to ignore some important general issues relating to the implementation of such co-operative policies. In this section we address some of these issues.

First, the above discussion shows that, mainly for reasons of analytical tractability, economists have tended to look at individual channels of transmission in theoretical models, or at single tools of economic policy. But do these partial snapshots of economic interdependence offer any useful insights into the likely gains or losses from co-operation 'in the real world'?

Second, we have not confronted the key question of how policy co-ordination (where this is desirable) can be implemented or sustained.

Finally, there is the theme common both to monetary and fiscal policy of conflict between the private sector and elected policy-makers. We have seen two types of problem here. We saw first that policy co-ordination may actually be undesirable because it enhances domestic distortions in the relationship between elected policy-makers and the private sector. Furthermore, schemes designed to achieve policy co-operation may run into difficulties when they have to fulfil the secondary role of alleviating domestic distortions. Here we highlighted the example of the dual role played by the ERM. The existence of a two-stage process of strategic interaction, involving at the one level governments with their electorate, and at a second level the two elected governments, raises the issue of whether institutional arrangements can be designed which deal in an optimal way with each problem. This is a crucial issue, but one which has received only limited attention.[22]

Partial models, uncertainty and co-operation in practice
Turning to the first point, do the types of partial analysis described so far offer any useful insights into the problems of policy co-ordination in reality? There are obvious dangers from concentrating on a subset of issues as is usually the case in simple analytical models. We can think of two cases of where this may matter. First, if there is agreement to co-operate in one sphere of policy or between a subset of countries in the world economy, is this to be encouraged, or is there a 'second-best theorem' which applies to international policy co-ordination whereby any partial solution is likely to be suboptimal? The second case is the existence of uncertainty. If policy-makers are uncertain about the nature of the macroeconomic linkages present, or disagree about the underlying structural model of the world economy, how does this affect the debate on co-operation?

The issue of whether partial agreements are desirable is ultimately an empirical question. Empirical evidence from macroeconometric models suggests that even between the main three OECD blocs (North America, Europe and Asia-Oceania) the spillover effects from policy may not be too large (see Bryant *et al.*, 1989). This suggests that policy co-ordination within each of these blocs may still be desirable if a wider agreement cannot be obtained, and that welfare gains from full co-operation at a global level may be small. A similar story applies to North–South macroeconomic interactions.[23] Again, the justification could be that North–South interactions are smaller in magnitude compared to intra-OECD linkages. But one should not be complacent about these findings. In some circumstances (e.g. the commodity price shocks of the 1970s, the Reagan–Volcker years in the early 1980s) macroeconomic shocks are large enough to reverberate throughout the world economy and the welfare gains from finding appropriate responses might be large. One should also not forget that small macroeconomic shocks can have persistent effects on long-term growth and employment performance, and that in the past macroeconometric models have been notoriously weak in their specification of the interactions between business cycles and growth.[24]

What about agreements that are limited in scope, in the sense that they focus solely on some intermediate objective such as exchange rate stabilization? Earlier we touched on this issue in the context of monetary policy co-ordination. In fact, where G7 summits have tended to encourage policy action, this has focused on commitments to co-operate on fostering exchange rate stability. The classic examples here are the G7 summits at the Plaza Hotel in September 1985 and the Louvre in February 1987 (see Funabashi, 1989). The question is whether this is beneficial. Hughes-Hallett *et al.* (1988) look at whether exchange rate stabilization is a good substitute for full policy co-ordination and show that such partial agreements may or may not deliver welfare gains – there is no guarantee. Earlier we saw that asymmetric exchange rate agreements such as the ERM could also come under pressure when the centre country is hit by a macroeconomic shock.

The recognition that individual policy instruments cannot be treated in isolation has led some economists to suggest 'rules' or 'blueprints' for the operation of the world economy which would have encouraged the implementation of a more symmetric system of policy co-ordination (see for example, Williamson, 1985; Williamson and Miller, 1987; McKinnon, 1988). Under McKinnon's proposal, the world monetary system would operate as a symmetric fixed nominal exchange rate system. Unlike the Gold Standard, domestic monetary policy would peg the price of a common basket of internationally traded goods. Fiscal policy would then be used by countries to attain external balance. The Williamson 'blueprint' proposals would instead focus monetary policy on a real exchange rate target, where the real exchange rate would be set consistently with medium-run current account balance.[25] Monetary policy on average in the world economy has to be set consistently with a global nominal income target. Fiscal policy is targeted through a combination of domestic demand growth targets and by estimating long-run sustainable capital flows.[26] The setting of real exchange rate targets, as noted by Williamson (1991; 1993) avoids the potential misalignments which result from nominal exchange rate adjustable pegs. Implicitly the argument is that a hard-ERM-type set-up cannot survive (even in the absence of asymmetric shocks of the type described above) if inflation in the follower countries does not adjust quickly enough.

The merits of various policy assignment schemes for fiscal and monetary policy have been scrutinized in the empirical literature (see, *inter alia*, Currie and Wren-Lewis, 1990; McKibbin and Sachs, 1989). However, a reorganization of the global monetary system is not on the agenda, and most recent G7 summits have concentrated more on monitoring and commenting on current macroeconomic conditions. Indeed, in recent years it is the political agenda of G7 meetings that has tended to grow rather than the economic agenda.

One thing which soon becomes apparent from such policy meetings is that policy-makers will rarely discuss matters such as macroeconomic policy co-ordination in isolation. Inevitably discussions of such matters become interrelated with other policy issues and major deals on macroeconomic policy co-ordination may be linked to other agreements. An example of this is the Bonn summit of 1978, where the expansionary fiscal package in Germany was linked with deals on oil taxation in the USA and Japanese trade liberalization (see Putnam and Bayne, 1987). Another example of such a link came with German protests over the post-1992 devaluations of the Italian lira and the pound sterling: there were thinly veiled suggestions that future membership of a single market should be linked to a commitment to maintain stable exchange rates, as the latter could be seen as an instrument of trade policy. All this suggests that, where deals are likely to be struck on macroeconomic policy co-ordination, the motives behind them might be different from those isolated in our simple partial analytical models. The political economy of the G7 summits may be such as to generate suboptimal politically motivated solutions such as those illustrated in the previous section, only on a wider scale, encompassing not only fiscal policy but also elements of trade policy, monetary policy and so on. Indeed, some see the German commitment to what turned out to be a fiscal overexpansion at the Bonn Summit in 1978 as an example of the problems behind such once-and-for-all initiatives.

So rule-based agreements may be preferred in order to avoid *ad hoc* politically motivated initiatives. However, as we have seen, such issue-based co-operation agreements have been confined to exchange rate policy and intervention in foreign exchange rate markets. Few countries are willing to enter into discussions of their fiscal affairs and to contemplate rule-based fiscal policy for the reasons discussed in our introduction. It is interesting that even the Maastricht criteria have not yet proved sufficient to trigger an adequate fiscal correction in those countries which are clearly keen to join EMU at the start (including France and Italy).

Some economists have suggested that the presence of uncertainty in policy co-ordination could explain why wide-ranging rule-based agreements on macroeconomic policy co-ordination are unlikely to be acceptable. Frankel and Rockett (1988) saw this as an important factor which would reduce welfare gains from co-ordination. Further studies have shown that this may work either way (see Gosh and Masson, 1994), but clearly the design of optimal rules under uncertainty becomes more complex and may explain why such agreements are unattainable. In this context, one should also perhaps stress the importance of information sharing which takes place at summit meetings.[27] This may facilitate policy agreements, and hence meetings between policy-makers might on balance be a good thing even if they do not seem to yield concrete agreements. Even here, however, there may be a counterargument if information sharing between politically motivated governments encourages the implementation of a policy co-ordination agreement which is undesirable from society's point of view.

So can we reach any positive conclusions on the scope of policy co-ordination agreements? The key conclusion is that ambitious all-embracing macroeconomic policy schemes are unlikely to work because of the constraints which they impose on policy-makers, because of the presence of uncertainty, and because the welfare gains are difficult to assess. This has led some commentators to suggest that policy co-operation is unlikely to be beneficial because it tends to be partial and occasional in nature, and because co-ordinated fiscal policy is unlikely to be considered (see Feldstein, 1988). However, this ignores the interrelationship between macroeconomic policy co-ordination and co-operation in other areas. For instance, one of the greatest achievements of the postwar era has arguably been the progressive move towards free trade. The close links between trade policy and exchange rate policy imply that lack of policy co-ordination on issues such as exchange rate stabilization might compromise major welfare gains in areas such as the pursuit of free trade. In the European context these tensions may become all too clear if a two-speed EMU were to emerge with greater exchange rate instability between core and periphery currencies.

Sustaining co-operative solutions

We now briefly turn to the issue of how co-operative international agreements could be sustained in practice, if they became desirable. Game theorists have looked towards various mechanisms to sustain reputational equilibria. In repeated games, punishment strategies are seen as important mechanisms. Policy-makers who repeatedly interact strategically will eventually learn to co-operate because the benefits of co-operation over a long period of time exceed the one-off benefits from breaking an agreement. Thus co-ordination can be sustained even in the absence of a legally binding agreement monitored by a supranational institution.[28]

Three factors militate against such equilibria emerging, however. The first is that the identity and political preferences of the players change (sometimes quite often) over time. Second, while it is easy to envisage punishment strategies devised over single policy outcomes, it seems unlikely that such mechanisms could sustain a complex rule-based agreement on co-ordinating fiscal and monetary policy. Once again, the conclusion would seem to be that one-off short-term policy decisions are easier to implement and sustain on the basis of each policy-maker's 'international reputation'. Instead it seems unlikely that a broad 'blueprint' proposal could be implemented unless the 'rules of the game' are clearly spelled out and monitored by an international institution such as the IMF.

Finally, the types of punishment strategy usually considered in the policy co-ordination literature to sustain reputational equilibria typically examine the two-country case. It seems even less likely that reputational forces could sustain co-ordination in a multi-player game where there are incentives for subgroups of players to deviate from the initial agreement, thereby reducing the 'loss of reputation'. The problems of reaching agreement between several parties are an important reason for the apparent sterility of many G7 summits. As Putnam and Bayne (1987) report, quite often successful 'blocking coalitions' can be formed which means that issues such as common fiscal policy actions are ruled out at the outset, as at Versailles[29] in 1982, and at Williamsburg in 1983.

The two-stage process of strategic interaction

Earlier we analysed at length the problem of domestic distortions in the policy co-ordination debate. It is clear that in the presence of a two-stage process of strategic interaction, policy co-ordination may enable the two policy-makers to collude against their respective electorates, and that this may make co-ordination undesirable.

We now briefly deal with recent attempts to address this problem. The key issue is whether institutional arrangements can be designed which can resolve the problem of domestic political distortions, and what effects these arrangements have on the incentives to co-operate.

Turning first to monetary policy, if one excludes reputational equilibria, there are essentially two possible approaches to tackling the problem of time inconsistency. The first, *delegation*, involves the appointment of a central banker whose preferences optimally reflect the preferences of society.[30] If each country were to appoint a 'conservative' central banker, would this solve the domestic credibility problem of each country and pave the way for useful policy co-ordination?[31]

Surprisingly, the answer to this question seems to be 'not necessarily'. Currie *et al.* (1995) show that if supply-side shocks are symmetric and there is unemployment persistence, it might actually be beneficial for countries to co-operate in selecting less conservative central bankers. There are potential losses, it seems, in each country 'putting its own house in order on inflation'.

A neater solution to the twin problem of credibility and co-ordination is provided by the second approach, *optimal contracts*. Taking the literature on optimal principal-agent contracts as a starting point, Persson and Tabellini (1993) and Walsh (1995) have shown how an appropriate contract could be drawn up for a central bank which overcomes the trade-off between achieving credibility and stabilization policy which was central to the delegation approach. Persson and Tabellini (1995) extend this notion to the problem of international policy co-ordination (see also Fershtman *et al.*, 1991), and show that an optimal performance contract can be devised for both central banks in a two-country model so as to implement a Pareto-optimal co-ordinated outcome. As pointed out by Persson and Tabellini, the importance of this result is that policy co-ordination would be enforced by *domestic* institutional arrangements, not by an *international agreement*, and would not raise problems of sustainability – neither country would have an incentive to deviate from the optimal contract.

The difficulty with performance contracts is that they seem to work in theory but they are rarely, if ever, observed in practice. This may be due to the fact that such contracts are complex and state-dependent.[32] Another reason might be that the inclusion of other sources of uncertainty (in addition to structural shocks), such as a changing trade-off between output and inflation, or changing preferences in society, might require a renegotiation of the optimal contract (see Muscatelli, 1995b)

In the area of fiscal policy, institutional arrangements to avoid domestic distortions (such as deficit spending limits) might make co-operation beneficial, but the trade-off is that there would be limits to any co-ordinated action.

Conclusions

As this is a broad survey, rather than summarizing all the points raised, it is more appropriate to conclude by highlighting two of the main themes. The first is that, although policy co-ordination cannot be expected to deliver clear-cut welfare gains, and although there are severe institutional constraints limiting the introduction of rule-based agreements on macroeconomic policy, one should be careful not to conclude that co-operation is counterproductive. *Ad hoc* one-off agreements on macroeconomic policy may well be politically motivated, but they may have as a counterpart continued co-operation in other areas of economic policy (such as trade) or in the political sphere which are clearly beneficial. Macroeconomists may have to accept that macroeconomic policy is sometimes treated as a 'side payment' in a wider co-operation game.

The second theme is that there is a two-stage strategic interaction: first between policy-makers and their electorate, and subsequently between policy-makers. This has interesting implications for the design of domestic and international institutions which economists have only recently begun to explore, but which should keep us talking about international policy co-ordination for many years to come.

Notes

1 For early contributions, see Kydland and Prescott (1977), Barro and Gordon (1983). For recent surveys, see Persson and Tabellini (1990) and Cukierman (1992).

2 See for instance Barro (1989), Blanchard (1985), Blanchard and Fischer (1989), and Frenkel and Razin (1987) for an open-economy application of intertemporal macroeconomics.

3 This forms the basis of the analysis in Cooper (1985).

4 Thus, R is the locus of points of tangency between the indifference map of country 1 and successive values of m^* (measured by a series of horizontal lines), while R* is the locus of points of tangency between the indifference map of country 2 and successive values of m (measured by a series of vertical lines).

5 Whether it does or not obviously depends on how much weight the policy-makers attach to each policy target; that is, whether they care more about the inflationary consequences of the oil price increase (which would tend to point to overcontraction) or whether they attach more weight to output stabilization (which would tend to create overexpansion) (see Oudiz and Sachs, 1984).

6 See also Stevenson *et al.* (1988) for a textbook analysis of the oil shock case.

7 For an early discussion of the $N - 1$ problem (the notion that in a fixed exchange rate regime between N countries only $N - 1$ monetary targets can be set independently), see Mundell (1968).

8 More recently there has been a reassessment of these early tests of German dominance. Von Hagen (1989) has suggested that sterilization tests might not fully capture the lagged impact from foreign exchange intervention on the domestic monetary base in Germany. De Grauwe (1988), Cohen and Wyplosz (1989) and Fratianni and Von Hagen (1990) conduct various types of tests of German dominance. Most of these authors look at the interdependence of interest rate and monetary base movements in the ERM countries to see whether the German domestic policy variables move independently of those in other countries and find that strong German dominance does not hold. However, there are potential problems with any simple test looking at the causal links between interest rate movements. The results might be affected by the presence of common explanatory factors in interest movements (e.g. the coincidence of the business cycle in Germany and its European neighbours). Furthermore, it is easy to understand why, in a fixed exchange rate system, a follower country with a weak currency might actually anticipate interest rate movements in the leader country. In any case, even if we do not choose to accept the extreme interpretation that monetary policy in the ERM was under Germany's exclusive control, the relevant point for our current discussion is that some element of asymmetry was surely present, which most commentators would be willing to accept.

9 This does raise the issue of what benefits accrue to the centre country as inflation will conceivably be higher in such a fixed exchange rate system. In fact greater exchange rate stability might yield considerable benefits for the tradable sector in the centre country by avoiding excessive short-run real appreciations (see Melitz, 1988). The trade-off facing Germany of slightly higher inflation for more stability in the real effective exchange rate might explain the Bundesbank's opposition to the setting up of the ERM (see Vaubel, 1980; Kloten, 1988) and is in essence a conflict between the objectives of the German government and its independent central bank.

10 The benefits in terms of a lower inflationary bias for the follower countries might even accrue if there are regular realignments of these countries due to some competitiveness objective (see Giavazzi and Pagano, 1988).

11 Some commentators would argue that German unification accelerated the decline of the hard-ERM regime which would have occurred in any case (see Williamson, 1991). This issue is discussed further below.

12 In order to keep the diagram simple, we have drawn it so that the two countries have symmetric preferences. However, one could easily adjust the initial position so that the centre country has a preference for lower inflation without affecting the results of this analysis.

13 This, of course, grossly oversimplifies the nature of the German unification shock, which did not consist merely of an exogenous impact on inflation, but involved a major fiscal impact. However, whether the reaction curve R shifts due to simple price level shock as in equation (2) or due to a shift in the preferences of the monetary authorities following a fiscal shock is immaterial from the point of view of the analysis which follows.

14 As in the case of the Hamada (1976; 1985) model, policy co-ordination problems emerge from the use of a single instrument to pursue mutually incompatible objectives.

15 For a contrary view which attributes differential labour market performance to institutional differences in labour markets, see Bean (1991) and Layard *et al.* (1991).

16 Once again, as for monetary policy, the results will depend upon the initial shock. It is intuitively obvious, however, that an exogenous increase in unemployment will trigger a fiscal stimulus in both countries which will only be limited by other considerations (a limit to fiscal expansion or a target for inflation).

17 One issue not analysed here in detail is the possible conflict and benefits from co-operation over the intertemporal terms of trade. In these models countries' fiscal policies can affect the world interest rate and attempt to push it in a direction that benefits them, depending on whether they are net debtors or net creditors (see Frenkel and Razin, 1987; Frenkel *et al.*, 1991; Buiter, 1987; Devereux, 1987). We do, however, touch on this issue below when discussing politically motivated deficits.

18 For an account of the Ricardian equivalence theorem, see Barro (1974; 1989) and Blanchard and Fischer (1989).

19 For an analysis of the role of capital shortage in the European economies, see also Dreze and Bean (1990).

20 The problem with traditional models of hysteresis based on insider–outsider considerations or on the role of the long-term unemployed (see Layard *et al.*, 1991) is that the length of the adjustment process towards the 'long-run NAIRU' in Europe seems to have lasted too long. This has pushed some economists to look to more structural interpretations of the unemployment problem based on considerations such as those of Phelps (1995) (see Manning, 1995).

21 As discussed in Phelps (1995), it is possible that a fiscal expansion in one country may increase equilibrium employment domestically while it decreases employment abroad. However, even if such an asymmetric effect is not present, a lack of co-ordination in fiscal policy may still generate a sub-optimal solution if each country ignores the contribution of its domestic debt on the world interest rate.

22 However, see Putnam (1988). Since writing the first draft of this chapter, I have become aware of Persson and Tabellini's (1995) survey, which makes a serious attempt at formalizing these issues. Some of their results are discussed below.

23 With a few exceptions (see Currie and Vines, 1988; Vines and Currie, 1995) this is an issue which has been neglected.

24 See Muscatelli and Vines (1989) and the contributions in Vines and Currie (1995) for an examination of the impact of Northern macroeconomic policy on the South's supply side.

25 For a discussion of the concept of a 'fundamental equilibrium exchange rate' (FEER), see Williamson (1985).

26 For an alternative assignment rule, see Boughton (1989).

27 Some authors distinguish between co-operation and co-ordination, treating the former as information exchange and the latter as agreements on common policies. However, in this survey we treat these two concepts as synonymous.

28 It could be argued that if reputational mechanisms are applicable, they are also likely to enforce co-operative outcomes between the private sector and the policy-maker, thus alleviating the time-inconsistency problem as in Barro and Gordon (1983). However, the problem with an atomistic private sector is that it cannot act strategically and it is not therefore apparent how a reputational equilibrium is chosen. Indeed what seems to be apparent from estimates of expected inflation obtained using bond yield differentials is that in countries where policy-makers have undergone a long struggle against inflation (e.g. France), inflationary expectations have fallen very gradually. This might suggest that the gains from building up one's reputation in the eyes of the private sector accrue more slowly. Where all the players in the game can act strategically, however, as in international policy co-ordination, a reputational equilibrium may have greater practical relevance.

29 The possibility of a fiscal expansion in Europe to counteract the effects of the Reagan fiscal expansion in the USA was discussed in the previous section. At Versailles, Mitterrand, whose party had espoused an expansionary policy when he came to power, was isolated and did not raise the issue. At Williamsburg, the anti fiscal-expansion coalition made up by the USA, Germany, Japan and the UK was sufficiently strong to block any discussion of this matter.

30 The delegation approach was introduced by Rogoff (1985b). In the presence of random aggregate supply shocks, it can be shown that the central banker who should be put in charge of monetary policy should be more 'conservative' on inflation than the median voter, but not totally oblivious to supply shocks. The literature on delegation has become more sophisticated with the introduction of delegation schemes where the central banker can be overridden at a cost (see Lohmann, 1992; Flood and Isard, 1990). These schemes can be shown, in some circumstances, to be superior to simple unconditional delegation (but see the caveat in Lossani *et al.*, 1995).

31 Indeed, monetary policy co-ordination might be easier between non-elected public servants whose planning horizon would be longer than that of elected politicians.

32 Lawyers often despair at economists' definitions of contracts. To most economists a contract is a solution to a problem; to a lawyer the contract *is* the problem.

References

Alesina, A. and Perotti, R. (1994). 'The political economy of budget deficits'. NBER Working Paper no. 4637.

Alesina, A. and Tabellini, G. (1990). 'A positive theory of fiscal deficits and government debt'. *Review of Economic Studies*, 57, 403–14.

Alogoskoufis, G. and Martin, C. (1991). 'External constraints on European unemployment'. In G. Alogoskoufis, L. Papademos and R. Portes (eds), *External Constraints on Macroeconomic Policy: The European Experience*. Cambridge: Cambridge University Press.

Alogoskoufis, G. and Varangis, P. (1992). 'OECD Fiscal policies and the relative price of primary commodities'. World Bank, IT Working Paper no. 955.

Barro, R. (1974). 'Are government bonds net wealth?' *Journal of Political Economy*, 82, 1095–1117.

Barro, R. (1989). 'The neoclassical approach to fiscal policy'. In R. Barro, (ed.), *Modern Business Cycle Theory*. Cambridge, MA: Harvard University Press.

Barro, R. and Gordon, D.B. (1983). 'Rules, discretion and reputation in a model of monetary policy'. *Journal of Monetary Economics*, 12, 101–21.

Bean, C. (1991). 'Comment on Alogoskoufis and Martin'. In G. Alogoskoufis, L. Papademos and R. Portes (eds), *External Constraints on Macroeconomic Policy: The European Experience*. Cambridge: Cambridge University Press.

Bean, C., Layard, R. and Nickell, S. (1986). 'The rise in unemployment: a multi-country study'. *Economica*, 53, S1–22.

Blanchard, O.J. (1985). 'Debt, deficits and finite horizons'. *Journal of Political Economy*, 93, 223–47.

Blanchard, O.J. (1987). 'Reaganomics'. *Economic Policy*, 2, 15–56

Blanchard, O.J. and Fischer, S. (1989). *Lectures in Macroeconomics*. Cambridge, MA: MIT Press.

Boughton, J.M. (1989). 'Policy assignment strategies with somewhat flexible exchange rates'. In B. Eichengreen, M. Miller and R. Portes (eds), *Blueprints for Exchange Rate Management*. Cambridge: Cambridge University Press.

Bruce, N. and Purvis, D. (1985). 'The specification and influence of goods and factor markets in open-economy macroeconomic models'. In R.W. Jones and P.B. Kenen (eds), *Handbook of International Economics*, Vol. 2. Amsterdam: North-Holland.

Bruno, M. (1991). 'High inflation and the nominal anchors of an open economy'. *Essays in International Finance*, no. 183, Princeton University, June.

Bruno, M. and Sachs, J. (1985). *The Economics of Worldwide Stagflation*. Oxford: Blackwell.

Bryant, R., Henderson, D., Holtham, G., Hooper, P. and Symanski, S. (eds) (1989). *Empirical Macroeconomics for Interdependent Economies.* Washington, DC: Brookings Institution.

Buiter, W. (1987). 'Fiscal policy in open interdependent economies'. In J. Frenkel and A. Razin (eds), *Economic Policy in Theory and Practice.* London: Macmillan.

Canzoneri, M.B. and Gray, J. (1985). 'Monetary policy games and the consequences of non-co-operative behaviour'. *International Economic Review*, 26, 547–64.

Canzoneri, M.B. and Henderson, D.W. (1988). 'Is sovereign policymaking bad?' *Carnegie-Rochester Series on Public Policy*, 28, 93–140.

Canzoneri, M.B. and Henderson, D.W. (1991). *Monetary Policy in Interdependent Economies: A Game-Theoretic Approach.* Cambridge, MA: MIT Press.

Cohen, D. and Wyplosz, C. (1989). 'The European Monetary Union: an agnostic evaluation'. In R.C. Bryant, D. Currie, J. Frenkel, P. Masson and R. Portes (eds), *Macroeconomic Policies in an Interdependent World.* Washington DC: IMF.

Cohen, D. and Wyplosz, C. (1990). 'Price and trade effects of exchange rate fluctuations and the design of policy co-ordination'. CEPR Discussion Paper no. 440.

Cohen, D. and Wyplosz, C. (1991). 'France and Germany in the EMS: the exchange rate constraint'. In G. Alogoskoufis, L. Papademos and R. Portes (eds), *External Constraints on Macroeconomic Policy: The European Experience.* Cambridge: Cambridge University Press.

Cooper, R.N. (1969). 'Macroeconomic policy adjustment in interdependent economies'. *Quarterly Journal of Economics*, 82, 1–24.

Cooper, R.N. (1985). 'Economic interdependence and co-ordination of economic policies'. In R.W. Jones and P.B. Kenen (eds), *Handbook of International Economics*, Vol. 2, Amsterdam: North-Holland.

Corden, M. (1993). 'Exchange rate policies for developing countries'. *Economic Journal*, 103, 198–207.

Cristini, A. (1995). 'Economic activity and commodity prices: theory and evidence'. In D. Vines and D. Currie, *North–South Linkages and International Macroeconomic Policy.* Cambridge: Cambridge University Press.

Cukierman, A. (1992). *Central Bank Strategy, Credibility and Independence: Theory and Evidence.* Cambridge, MA: MIT Press.

Currie, D. and Vines, D. (eds) (1988). *Macroeconomic Interactions between North and South.* Cambridge: Cambridge University Press.

Currie, D. and Wren-Lewis, S. (1990). 'Evaluating the extended target zone proposal for the G3'. *Economic Journal*, 100, 105–23.

Currie, D., Levine, P. and Pearlman, J. (1995). 'Can delegation be counterproductive? The choice of "conservative" bankers in open economies'. CEPR Discussion Paper no. 1148, March.

De Grauwe, P. (1988). 'Is the European monetary system a DM-zone?' CEPR Discussion Paper no. 297, March.

Delors Report (1989). *Report on Economic and Monetary Union in the European Community.* Luxembourg: Office for Official Publications of the European Communities.

Devereux, M. (1987). 'Fiscal spending, the terms of trade, and real interest rates'. *Journal of International Economics*, 22, 1–23.

Drazen, A. and Masson, P. (1994). 'Credibility of policies versus credibility of policymakers'. *Quarterly Journal of Economics*, 107, 735–54.

Dreze, J. and Bean, C. (eds) (1990). *Europe's Unemployment Problem.* Cambridge, MA: MIT Press.

Eichengreen, B., Rose, A. and Wyplosz, C. (1995a). 'Speculative attacks on pegged exchange rates'. CEPR Discussion Paper no. 1060.

Eichengreen, B., Tobin, J. and Wyplosz, C. (1995b). 'Two cases for sand in the wheels of international finance'. *Economic Journal*, 105, 162–72.

Ermisch, J. and Muscatelli, A. (1993). 'Migration and macroeconomic stability in a monetary union'. Paper presented at CEPR workshop on International Migration, Konstanz, 26–27 February.

Feldstein, M. (1988). 'Thinking about policy co-ordination'. *Journal of Economic Perspectives*, 2, 3–13.

Fershtman, C., Judd, K. and Kalai, E. (1991). 'Observable contracts: strategic delegation and co-operation'. *International Economic Review*, 32, 551–9.

Flood, R.P. and Isard, P. (1990). 'Monetary policy strategies'. NBER Working Paper no. 2770.

Frankel, J. and Rockett, K. (1988). 'International macroeconomic co-ordination when policymakers disagree on the model'. *American Economic Review*, 78, 318–40.

Fratianni, M. and Von Hagen, J. (1990). 'Asymmetries and realignments in the EMS'. In P. De Grauwe and L. Papademos (eds), *The European Monetary System in the 1990s.* London: Longman.

Frenkel, J. and Johnson, H.G. (eds) (1976). *The Monetary Approach to the Balance of Payments*. London: Allen & Unwin.

Frenkel, J. and Johnson, H.G. (eds) (1978). *The Economics of Exchange Rates: Selected Studies*. Reading, MA: Addison-Wesley.

Frenkel, J. and Razin, A. (1987). *Fiscal Policies and the World Economy* (2nd ed.). Cambridge, MA: MIT Press.

Frenkel, J., Razin, A. and Sadka, E. (1991). *International Taxation in an Integrated World.* Cambridge, MA: MIT Press.

Funabashi, Y. (1989). *Managing the Dollar: From the Plaza to the Louvre.* Washington, DC: IIE.

Giavazzi, F. and Giovannini, A. (1987). 'Models of the EMS: is Europe a greater Deutsche-Mark area?' In R. Bryant and R. Portes (eds), *Global Macroeconomics: Policy Conflicts and Co-operation*. London: Macmillan.

Giavazzi, F. and Giovannini, A. (1989). *Limiting Exchange Rate Flexibility*. Cambridge, MA: MIT Press.

Giavazzi, F. and Pagano, M. (1988). 'The advantage of tying one's hand: EMS discipline and central bank credibility'. *European Economic Review*, 32, 1055–75.

Gosh, A. and Masson, P. (1994). *Economic Co-operation in an Uncertain World*. Oxford: Blackwell.

Hamada, K. (1974). 'Alternative exchange rate systems and the interdependence of monetary policies'. In R. Aliber (ed.), *National Monetary Policies and the International Financial System*. Chicago: University of Chicago Press.

Hamada, K. (1976). 'A strategic analysis of monetary interdependence'. *Journal of Political Economy*, 84, 677–700.

Hamada, K. (1979). 'Macroeconomic strategy and co-ordination under alternative exchange rates'. In R. Dornbusch and J. Frenkel (eds), *International Economic Policy*. Baltimore, MD: Johns Hopkins University Press.

Hamada, K. (1985). *The Political Economy of International Monetary Interdependence*. Cambridge, MA: MIT Press.

Hughes-Hallett, A.J., Holtham, G. and Hutson, G. (1988). 'Exchange rate targeting as a surrogate for international policy co-ordination'. In B. Eichengreen, M. Miller and R. Portes (eds), *Blueprints for Exchange Rate Management*. Cambridge: Cambridge University Press.

Kenen, P.B. (1988). 'Reflections on the EMS experience'. In F. Giavazzi, S. Micossi and M. Miller (eds), *The European Monetary System*. Cambridge: Cambridge University Press.

Kloten, N. (1988). 'Die europäische Wahrungsintegration: Chancen und Risiken'. *Deutsche Bundesbank Auszüge aus Presseartikeln*, 82, 1–7.

Kydland, F. and Prescott, E.C. (1977). 'Rules rather than discretion: the inconstancy of optimal plans'. *Journal of Political Economy*, 84, 473–91.

Layard, R., Nickell, S.J. and Jackman, R. (1991). *Unemployment: Macroeconomic Performance and the Labour Market*. Oxford: Oxford University Press.

Levine, P. and Currie, D. (1987). 'Does international policy co-ordination pay and is it sustainable? A two-country analysis'. *Oxford Economic Papers*, 39, 38–74.

Lockwood, B., Miller, M. and Zhang, L. (1993). 'Delegating monetary policy when unemployment persists'. Mimeo, University of Warwick.

Lohmann, S. (1992). 'The optimal degree of commitment: credibility versus flexibility'. *American Economic Review*, 82, 273–86.

Lossani, M., Natale, P.G. and Tirelli, P. (1995). 'Incomplete information in monetary policy games: rules rather than a conservative central banker'. Mimeo, Università Cattolica, Milan.

Manning, A. (1995). 'Developments in labour market theory and their implications for macroeconomic policy'. *Scottish Journal of Political Economy*, 42, 250–66.

Mastropasqua, C., Micossi, S. and Rinaldi, R. (1988). 'Interventions, sterilisation and monetary policy in European Monetary System countries, 1979–87'. In F. Giavazzi, S. Micossi and M. Miller (eds), *The European Monetary System*. Cambridge: Cambridge University Press.

McKibbin, W. and Sachs, J. (1989). 'Implications of policy rules for the world economy'. In R.C. Bryant, D. Currie, J. Frenkel, P. Masson and R. Portes (eds), *Macroeconomic Policies in an Interdependent World*. Washington, DC: IMF.

McKinnon, R. (1988). 'Monetary and exchange rate policies for international financial stability'. *Journal of Economic Perspectives*, 2, 83–103.

Melitz, J. (1988). 'Monetary discipline and co-operation in the European Monetary System: a synthesis'. In F. Giavazzi, S. Micossi and M. Miller (eds), *The European Monetary System*. Cambridge: Cambridge University Press.

Mundell, R. (1968). *International Economics*, New York: Macmillan.

Muscatelli, V.A. (1995a). 'Comment on Cristini'. In D. Vines and D. Currie, *North–South Linkages and International Macroeconomic Policy*. Cambridge: Cambridge University Press.

Muscatelli, V.A. (1995b). 'Designing monetary institutions under uncertainty: the value of the status quo'. University of Glasgow Discussion Paper.

Muscatelli, V.A. and Vines, D. (1989). 'Macroeconomic interactions between the North and the South'. In R.C. Bryant, D. Currie, J. Frenkel, P. Masson and R. Portes (eds), *Macroeconomic Policies in an Interdependent World*. Washington, DC: IMF.

Newell, A. and Symons, J. (1985). 'Wages and employment in the OECD countries'. Centre for Labour Economics, Discussion Paper no. 219, LSE.

Obstfeld, M. and Rogoff, K. (1994). 'Exchange rate economics redux'. NBER Working Paper no. 4693, April.

Oudiz, G. and Sachs, J. (1984). 'Macroeconomic policy co-ordination and the industrial economies'. *Brookings Papers on Economic Activity*, 1, 1–64.

Persson, T. and Svensson, L. (1989). 'Why a stubborn conservative would run a deficit'. *Quarterly Journal of Economics*, 104, 325–45.

Persson, T. and Tabellini, G. (1990). *Macroeconomic Policy, Credibility and Politics*. Chur: Harwood Academic Publishers.

Persson, T. and Tabellini, G. (1993). 'Designing institutions for monetary stability'. *Carnegie-Rochester Conference Series on Public Policy*, 39.

Persson, T. and Tabellini, G. (1994). 'Introduction'. In *Monetary and Fiscal Policy: Vol 2: Politics*. Cambridge, MA: MIT Press.

Persson, T. and Tabellini, G. (1995). 'Double-edged incentives: institutions and policy co-ordination'. CEPR Discussion Paper no. 1141.

Phelps, E.S. (1995). *Structural Slumps*. Cambridge, MA: Harvard University Press.

Putnam, R. (1988). 'Diplomacy and domestic politics: the logic of two-level games'. *International Organisation*, 42, 427–60.

Putnam, R. and Bayne, N. (1987). *Hanging Together: Co-operation and Conflict in the Seven-Power Summits*. Cambridge, MA: Harvard University Press.
Rogoff, K. (1985a). 'Can international monetary policy co-ordination be counterproductive?' *Journal of International Economics*, 18, 199–217.
Rogoff, K. (1985b). 'The optimal degree of commitment to an intermediate monetary target'. *Quarterly Journal of Economics*, 100, 1169–90.
Sachs, J. (1985). 'The dollar and the policy mix'. *Brookings Papers on Economic Activity*, 1, 117–98.
Sachs, J. (1986). 'The Bolivian hyperinflation and stabilisation'. NBER Working Paper no. 2073.
Stevenson, A., Muscatelli, V.A. and Gregory, M. (1988). *Macroeconomic Theory and Stabilisation Policy*. London: Philip Allan.
Tabellini, G. (1990). 'Domestic policies and the international co-ordination of fiscal policies'. *Journal of International Economics*, 28, 245–65.
Tabellini, G. and Alesina, A. (1990). 'Voting on the budget deficit'. *American Economic Review*, 80, 37–49.
Vaubel, R. (1980). 'The return to the new EMS'. *Carnegie-Rochester Series on Public Policy*, 13, 173–221.
Vaubel, R. (1985). 'International collusion or competition for macroeconomic policy co-ordination'. *Recherches Economiques de Louvain*, 51, 223–40.
Vines, D. and Currie, D. (1995). *North–South Linkages and International Macroeconomic Policy*. Cambridge: Cambridge University Press.
Von Hagen, J. (1989). 'Monetary targeting with exchange rate constraints: the Bundesbank in the 1980s'. Working Paper, Federal Reserve Bank of St Louis.
Walsh, C. (1995). 'Optimal contracts for central bankers'. *American Economic Review*, 85, 150–67.
Williamson, J. (1985). *The Exchange Rate System*. Washington, DC: Institute for International Economics.
Williamson, J. (1991). 'FEERs and the ERM'. *National Institute Economic Review*, August.
Williamson, J. (1993). 'Exchange rate management'. *Economic Journal*, 103, 188–97.
Williamson, J. and Miller, M. (1987). *Targets and Indicators: A Blueprint for International Co-ordination of Economic Policy*. Washington, DC: Institute for International Economics.

Index

Note: 'n.' after a page reference indicates the number of a note on that page.